How Washington Actually Works

FOR

DUMMIES®

WILEY

John Wiley & Sons, Inc.

P9-ELO-057

How Washington Actually Works For Dummies®
Published by
John Wiley & Sons, Inc.
111 River St.
Hoboken, NJ 07030-5774
www.wiley.com

WILEY

Acknowledgments

We would like to acknowledge the generous contributions of time and expertise from the C&M International team in the preparation of this book, and in particular Doral Cooper, Peter Allgeier, Joshua Boswell, Paul Burkhead, Kate Clemans, Melissa Coyle, Paul Davies, Ke Ji, Andrew Tein, Christopher Wilson, and Patty Wu.

C&M International is an international and regulatory consultancy in Washington, D.C., and is affiliated with Crowell & Moring LLP, an international law firm representing clients in litigation and arbitration, regulatory and transactional matters, with offices in Washington, D.C., New York, Los Angeles, San Francisco, Orange County, London, and Brussels.

Publisher's Acknowledgments

Project Editor: Joan Friedman

Acquisitions Editor: Tracy Boggier

Cover Photo: © iStockphoto.com / Dwight Nadig

Cartoons: Rich Tennant (www.the5thwave.com)

Project Coordinator: Kristie Rees

Table of Contents

Introduction

*W*ashington, D.C., Capital of the Free World. The most powerful city on Earth. No other country, company, or international organization can compare with the reach and wealth of the U.S. federal government. Policymaking — the art of deciding what programs to support, what laws to pass, or what regulations to write — is at the core of what Washington does and is what everyone, from the President on down, wants to influence. The Founding Fathers expected policymaking to be an inclusive process, and the diversity and number of actors who have emerged in Washington reflect this reality. While civics textbooks can teach you how a bill becomes law, a textbook is little help in understanding how things really get done in Washington.

As with any complicated system, you can easily miss the forest for the trees when trying to figure out policymaking. But don't despair! You *can* get a grip on the policymaking process at the federal level — the players, the rules, and the game they play — without knowing the minutiae of congressional procedure or the agency behind every acronym. In fact, with a firm grasp of the basics, you too can try your hand at the policymaking game.

What will you learn from following pages? You won't get a dry explanation of the American system of government (you remember that from grade school anyway, right?). Instead, you find a playbook for how Washington really works: who has a seat at the table, how the policymaking process works, and how someone survives. We give you the inside skinny. Some disillusioned observers may call the whole process dysfunctional, and some critics may decry it as corrupt, but for the veterans who have witnessed its successes and failures, it's simply how Washington actually works.

About This Book

As any tourist knows, finding your way around the city of Washington, D.C., can be a challenge. Finding your way around Washington's policymaking world is even more harrowing. It has confounded fresh-out-of-college interns and newly elected presidents equally.

This book is your map to understanding the intricate world of federal policymaking. We introduce you to all the major players, from federal bureaucrats and Congress to lobbyists and the media, and we share our insights about how much power each group actually wields. We also offer a few tips for connecting with these players, in case your goal in reading this book is to set yourself on a course for becoming one of D.C.'s most influential.

As with any *For Dummies* book, this is a reference book, so feel free to jump from chapter to chapter to satisfy your curiosity and read what's most relevant to you.

Conventions Used in This Book

To help you navigate this text, we use the following conventions:

- ✔ When we introduce a new term, it appears in *italic* and we provide a definition or explanation nearby.

- ✔ Sometimes we share interesting information that isn't crucial to your understanding of the topic at hand. That information appears in a *sidebar* — a gray box set apart from the rest of the text.

- ✔ Website addresses appear in monofont so they're easy to pick out if you need to go back and find them.

Foolish Assumptions

We wrote this book assuming that you're interested in understanding the behind-the-scenes world of how things get done in Washington. Perhaps you are a cable news junkie who gets tired of watching hours of programming that merely touch the superficial and trivial side of Washington politics. You may be a civic-minded citizen who desires to become more involved in influencing federal policy. Maybe you're a student studying U.S. politics who wonders how things really get done. Or you could even be an old Washington hand who is amused to find a book about daily life in the capital. Whoever you are, the fact that you are reading these words right now indicates an above-average intelligence and insatiable curiosity about politics.

Icons Used in This Book

Throughout the book, we place two icons in the margins that call your attention to certain types of text. Here's what each icon means:

This icon denotes paragraphs that contain useful how-to's for better understanding how Washington works and positioning yourself for a D.C. career.

When you see this icon, pay close attention. The point we're making is something that's worth recalling long after you read the words.

Where to Go from Here

The great thing about this book is you can start anywhere you want. Feel free to use the table of contents to pinpoint subjects of particular interest.

If you're aiming for a career as a federal worker, you may want to head straight to Chapter 2. If the President's job is particularly fascinating to you, aim for Chapter 6. If you want to know if this book confirms your cynical view of special interests, Chapter 3 on lobbying may be right for you. The civic-minded reader may want to jump to Chapter 8 to find out how to start participating in American political life.

Wherever you start, remember to come back and page through the chapters you skip — we happen to think they're all worthwhile!

"We appreciate your personal and financial backing of this bill. However, Congress is reluctant to name it after you. I'm sure you understand, Mr. Hairbrane."

Chapter 1

A Brief History of Washington

● ●

In This Chapter

▶ Choosing the capital's location and building it from scratch

▶ Growing into the city we recognize today

▶ Considering the government's growth in the past century

▶ Tracking the city's demographic trends

▶ Appreciating the power of the Washington establishment

● ●

*M*ore than the capital of a great nation, Washington, D.C., is the political nerve center of the last (at least for now) remaining superpower, as well as a center of global diplomacy and, increasingly, the world of high-tech business. While this book focuses primarily on Washington's policymaking role as the seat of the federal government, it is also about the institutions and individuals that define the city. To understand how Washington became the unique place it is today, in this chapter we take a step back in time to its origins as a city and capital.

Becoming the National Capital

When the 13 colonies declared their independence from the British Empire in July 1776, Washington the city did not exist. Washington the man was encamped with the Continental Army in New York, years away from winning the war and still more than a decade away from becoming the nation's first president.

Commonwealth? State? What's the difference?

Why is Virginia a commonwealth and Maryland a state? Virginia is one of four states in the Union that has designated itself a commonwealth. The other three are Kentucky, Massachusetts, and Pennsylvania.

These four states wanted to emphasize that their government is based on the people's common consent. Absolutely no constitutional distinction exists between commonwealths and states.

But by the early 1790s, a new city was under construction on the Potomac, and at the dawn of the 19th century the federal government would relocate to its new and permanent seat in Washington, D.C. In this section, we explain how the nation's capital came into being.

Putting D.C. on the map

The land on which Washington is built lies on the East Coast of the United States along the Potomac River, which separates it from the Commonwealth of Virginia. On its other three sides the city is surrounded by the state of Maryland.

Listening to the city's residents today, you won't hear many southern accents. But Washington is undeniably a southern city, located below the Mason-Dixon Line; a two-hour ride down I-95 takes you to the once-Confederate capital of Richmond. (President John F. Kennedy, not kindly, once described Washington as "A city of southern efficiency and northern charm.") Washington's southern location, as you will soon find out, was central to its selection for the nation's new capital.

Building Georgetown and Alexandria

The earliest inhabitants of this land were Native Americans, but by the 17th century, Europeans had arrived. For these settlers, tobacco was king, and the trade of this commodity on the Potomac led to the founding of the federal district's first two major settlements: Georgetown and Alexandria.

Best known today for its prestigious university, rows of expensive townhouses for the D.C. elite, and swanky shops, Georgetown was located in what would become the northwest quadrant of the District of Columbia. It originally fell within the bounds of Frederick County, Maryland. In 1751, the Maryland Legislature authorized a group of commissioners to purchase 60 acres of land along the Potomac River from owners George Gordon and George Beall. The commissioners were instructed to plan and construct a new town called Georgetown. George II was the sovereign at the time, but history isn't clear about which of the many Georges the town name honors. Georgetown quickly grew into a bustling commercial port, as it was fortuitously located on a key route for tobacco shipments from Maryland and was also the farthest navigable point on the Potomac for ocean-going ships.

Alexandria, located south of Georgetown on the Virginia side of the Potomac, had similar beginnings. In response to a petition by land speculators with the Ohio Company, in 1749 the House of Burgesses (the colonists' first elected assembly of representatives) approved the establishment of Alexandria at the site of a tobacco warehouse just north of Huntington Creek, a tributary of the Potomac. The Ohio Company considered the area ideal for a port that could facilitate the trade it hoped to pursue deeper inland. (Fun fact: Two maps of the area as it existed prior to the construction of Alexandria were prepared by a young surveyor named George Washington.)

Sitting far from the early seats of power

The establishment of Washington as the capital of the fledgling United States was certainly not inevitable. The area of the future District of Columbia consisted of a few small communities founded because they were convenient places to ship and store tobacco. The common belief that Washington was built on a swamp has received significant pushback from historians. (They prefer the term *tidal marsh*, thank you very much.) Regardless, the Founding Fathers must have had admirable amounts of imagination to picture a new Rome rising from its muddy shores. (They certainly tried hard: At the time of Washington's founding, the small Goose Creek, a tributary that flowed near Capitol Hill, was grandiosely renamed the Tiber.)

The great political events of the American Revolution occurred far from the future capital. Both the First and Second Continental Congresses met chiefly (though not exclusively) in the already established city of Philadelphia. Under the Articles of Confederation, members of the Congress of the Confederation met successively in Philadelphia, Princeton, Annapolis, Trenton, and New York City.

National politics might have happily ignored the lonely banks on the Potomac had it not been for the failure of the Articles of Confederation to manage the fractious colonies-turned-states. But because the Articles purposely gave the Confederation Congress no real power, some states began taking matters into their own hands.

Meeting in Mount Vernon and Annapolis

In order to better regulate the Potomac River, Pocomoke River, and Chesapeake Bay, Virginia and Maryland decided in 1785 to send a group of delegates to meet in Alexandria and sort out the situation. George Washington, by now a famous (albeit retired) general, invited the delegates to continue their work at Mount Vernon, his nearby plantation. Due to Washington's hospitality, the interstate gathering became known as the Mount Vernon Conference, and the agreement the delegates arrived at became the Mount Vernon Compact.

A shining success for interstate diplomacy, the Mount Vernon Conference served as a model for the following year's Annapolis Convention, at which a dozen delegates from various states met in Maryland to discuss the defects of the federal government, specifically related to interstate trade. The gathering in Annapolis was followed by the historic Constitutional Convention of 1787, where state delegates met in Philadelphia to deliberate on a new framework for the national government.

What had begun as a small gathering in Alexandria in 1785 culminated in the drafting of the U.S. Constitution, which set the stage for the eventual establishment of Washington, D.C. Article I, Section 8 of the Constitution lists the powers of Congress, including this one:

> To exercise exclusive Legislation in all Cases whatsoever, over such District (not exceeding ten Miles square) as may, by Cession of particular States, and the Acceptance of Congress, become the Seat of the Government of the United States . . .

Wheeling and dealing

Some capitals emerge from the eternal depths of history. Legend has it that Washington, D.C., was the result of a back-room political compromise. President Washington, newly sworn into office at New York's Federal Hall in 1789, faced a daunting challenge: War had strained the colonies' finances to the breaking point, and the young nation was deeply in debt. Creditors were clamoring to be paid. Much of the debt was owed by individual states, but Alexander Hamilton, Secretary of the Treasury in the new Washington administration, had a plan. In his First Report on Public Credit, delivered to Congress in January 1790, Hamilton proposed that the national government fully assume the debts of the states.

Hamilton's proposal was met with swift opposition, led by Secretary of State Thomas Jefferson and James Madison, a member of the House of Representatives from Virginia. The two men leveled three main lines of attack:

- ✔ By this point, the debt was held largely by speculators who, in many cases, had bought it from desperate soldiers for far below its original value. Thus, speculators would profit at the expense of the heroes of the American Revolution.

- ✔ As everyone recognized, the assumption of the states' debts would greatly increase the power of the federal government because subsequently all creditors would look to one central authority for repayment, necessitating that the federal government raise revenues.

✔ The debts themselves were not evenly distributed among the states. Some southern states, Virginia among them, had already paid most of their war-era debts. Others, including several northern states, had paid little and were still struggling financially. If the federal government assumed responsibility for all state debts and began collecting federal taxes, states like Virginia would essentially be forced to help pay off the debts of the less financially disciplined states.

Hamilton needed a deal to get around this political impasse. With Jefferson's help, a bargain was struck in which Madison, both a Virginian and the most influential member of the House, would help get Hamilton the votes needed to pass the Funding Act, which would allow the federal government to assume the states' debts. In exchange, Hamilton would help Madison get the votes needed to pass the Residence Act, which would fix the site of the national capital along the Potomac River, thereby giving the South increased political power to balance the North's growing economic power. The decision on the capital's final location would be left to President Washington. In essence, the capital would be the reward for acquiescing to the debt deal — not a pretty beginning, but a harbinger of political deal-making to come.

What's in a name?

Article I, Section 8 of the Constitution refers to a "District" that should serve as the "Seat of the Government of the United States." The first commissioners who supervised the development of the city decided to name the whole 100-square-mile area the *Territory of Columbia* or *District of Columbia* and the new town they were planning the *City of Washington* (after President George Washington). At the time, the City of Washington was not the only town within the District; Georgetown and Alexandria also fell within its boundaries. Congress returned Alexandria to Virginia in 1846 and merged Georgetown and the City of Washington in 1871. Since that time, the terms *Washington* and *District of Columbia* (or just *D.C.*) have gradually become interchangeable in normal conversation. While the latter remains the federal district's official name, the former is more commonly used.

On January 24, 1791, acting under the authority granted to him by the Residence Act, President Washington issued a proclamation fixing the boundaries of the new federal district. The capital would be a square measuring 10 miles on each side, although oriented on a map it would appear in the shape of a diamond. It would include 69 square miles of Maryland territory (including Georgetown) and 31 square miles of Virginia territory (including Alexandria). All that remained to be done was build a city from scratch.

Designing the national capital

The design and beauty of Washington as it exists today largely reflect the original plans of a Frenchman, Pierre Charles L'Enfant. As a young artist and engineer, he had followed in the footsteps of another Frenchman, American Revolutionary General Lafayette: L'Enfant joined the Continental Army and served under Washington in the Revolutionary War, including during the infamous winter at Valley Forge.

L'Enfant clearly impressed Washington, who in 1791 chose him to design the new capital. On March 9, 1791, L'Enfant arrived in Georgetown to begin surveying, and soon thereafter he presented his "Plan of the city intended for the permanent seat of the government of the United States."

The plan sketched by L'Enfant (a revised version of which is shown in Figure 1-1) envisaged Washington much as it exists today. The city would be a grid of north–south and east–west streets, with avenues traveling diagonally across and intersecting the grid at several large open spaces. The Capitol building in which Congress would meet would be built on Jenkins Hill (now Capitol Hill), with the future Pennsylvania Avenue connecting it to the President's house. From the Capitol directly west would run a mile-long, garden-lined grand avenue that would end just south of the presidential residence.

Political disagreements with commissioners and others prevented L'Enfant from seeing his grand plan implemented. However, today's Washington reflects the bold imagination and spirit of Pierre Charles L'Enfant.

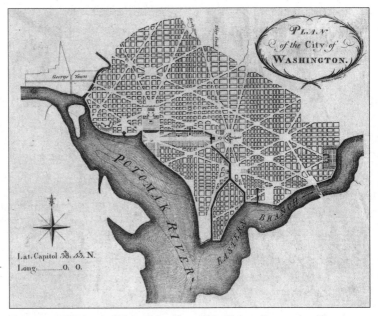

Figure 1-1: L'Enfant's "Plan of the City of Washington" as revised by city planner Andrew Ellicott.

After years of political wrangling, backroom dealing, and professional rivalries, Washington's boundaries were drawn and its street map completed. By the end of the 18th century, construction could finally commence.

Watching the City Develop

This little book is really about the Washington, D.C., of today, so we won't dwell on the fascinating history of the city (which has been detailed exhaustively elsewhere). Instead, here we quickly run through a couple centuries, with an eye toward understanding the Washington of today.

The federal government stayed in Philadelphia as the new capital in Washington was being constructed. On May 15, 1800, President John Adams ordered the federal government to relocate to Washington, and the Adams family became the first First Family to live in what today we call the White House. "I pray Heaven to bestow the best of Blessings on this House and all that shall hereafter inhabit it," he said upon moving in. "May none but honest and wise men ever rule under this roof."

Things did not remain tranquil for long. Two years into the War of 1812, the British occupied Washington and burned down many of its most prominent public buildings, including the U.S. Capitol, White House, and Library of Congress. The former two survived only as burnt-out shells; the latter survived thanks to Thomas Jefferson's offer to replace the 3,000 books lost in the fire with his own personal library of some 6,500 books, thereby doubling the Library of Congress's size and vastly expanding the variety of books in its possession. (Jefferson had a motive for his munificence; he was, as always, deeply in debt and needed the $24,000 Congress paid him.) For a time, Congress considered relocating back to Philadelphia, but in the end it decided to stay and rebuild.

Washington's public buildings were repaired, and slowly the city began adding to its array of famous edifices, monuments, and museums. Construction of the Washington Monument began in 1848 and was completed some three decades later. In the meantime, the U.S. Capitol got its iconic dome, which (as you may recall from your grade school textbook) stood conspicuously unfinished at Lincoln's inauguration in 1861. Washington even got its famous National Zoo in 1889. Nonetheless, Washington did lose one major element of its original design: The town of Alexandria voted in favor of "retrocession" in 1846 and, with President James K. Polk's signature, was ceded back to Virginia. (Proponents argued that the town received little advantage from being part of the capital and would benefit from greater investment as part of Virginia.)

Ahead of Washington's centennial in 1900, a Senate commission chaired by Senator James McMillan developed a new park system for the city. Among its most important decisions, the McMillan Commission called for a relandscaping of the National Mall (including the removal of a railroad station and tracks) into an open greenway, re-creating to a certain degree L'Enfant's original design. Another result of the McMillan Commission was the construction of Union Station, Washington's main train station, which opened in 1908 just blocks away from the U.S. Capitol.

Throughout the 1800s and into the 1900s, Washington experienced a phenomenal population explosion. A small town of just 8,144 residents in 1800 was transformed into a small city of 486,869 residents by 1930, at which point it was roughly two-thirds White and one-third African American. The city has always had a strong African American population, which was initially the result of slavery but was bolstered during Reconstruction in part thanks to federal employment opportunities and educational institutions like Howard University.

Growing the Government in the 20th Century

The days are long gone when growth in Washington, D.C., was viewed in terms of just physical construction. Enter politics.

In this section, we shift attention toward how and when the federal government grew into the entity we recognize today.

The Roosevelt Years: The New Deal and World War II

Although the City of Washington grew throughout the 1800s and early 1900s, the federal government did not expand greatly in size and scope. The election of President Franklin D. Roosevelt in 1932, however, put the government on a new trajectory. Roosevelt's New Deal legislative program not only reshaped the role of government in the lives of Americans but also reshaped the federal bureaucracy and the city in which it was based. The buildup during World War II caused even further federal expansion.

A review of the many agencies that collectively constitute today's federal bureaucracy underlines the far-reaching legacy of the New Deal. The Social Security Administration, Securities and Exchange Commission, Federal Deposit Insurance Corporation, Federal Housing Administration, and National Labor Relations Board are but a few of the government entities that were first established as part of the New Deal expansion. Other programs — the Civilian Conservation Corps, Public Works Administration, and Works Progress Administration — were only temporary but also helped establish a new precedent for the size and reach of the federal government.

The creation of so many new departments and agencies led to an obvious problem: The city didn't have enough office space for everyone. Laws preventing skyscrapers in Washington, D.C., magnified the issue. (Although the popular conception is that no building in Washington may be taller than the Washington Monument, in fact a 1910 law prohibits buildings in Washington from being more than 20 feet higher than the width of the city street on which they are built. Periodic attempts to relax these restrictions have been unsuccessful so far.)

One result of this office space shortage was the construction of the Pentagon across the Potomac in Arlington to house the Department of War (later Defense). With a powerful display of American competitive spirit, the government ended up constructing the largest office building in the world, which the Pentagon remains to this day. Ironically, construction of this symbol of U.S. military might began on September 11, 1941 — 60 years to the day before terrorists flew a plane into the Pentagon in an effort to destroy that symbol.

From the Cold War to the new millennium

Between the end of World War II and the beginning of the Cold War, new demands to protect American security arose. President Harry S. Truman signed the National Security Act of 1947, which reorganized the entire U.S. military establishment and established the National Security Council and the Central Intelligence Agency (the successor to World War II's swash-buckling Office of Strategic Services).

Many more additions to the federal bureaucracy followed. Here are just some examples that span the second half of the 20th century:

- In 1958, President Dwight D. Eisenhower established the National Aeronautics and Space Administration (NASA).

- In the 1960s, President Lyndon B. Johnson's Great Society legislation introduced such federal programs as Medicare and Medicaid, the National Endowment for the Arts, the National Endowment for the Humanities, and the Department of Transportation.

- The latest wave of government expansion took place post 9/11. Once again, security concerns drove growth. President George W. Bush created the Department of Homeland Security, as well as the ubiquitous Transportation Security Administration (and airport security lines — and personal privacy issues). A new layer of bureaucracy, the Office of the Director of National Intelligence, was laid on top of the 16-member intelligence community.

Eyeing D.C. Today

The City of Washington is still readily recognizable from L'Enfant's early sketches, but it's a far different place from the rural fields and marshes he saw in the late 18th century. Washington has weathered more than two centuries of history, all the while growing in size and bureaucracy. It has also become one of the most desirable places to live in the United States, with among the highest income and education levels in the country. No matter how much trouble Washington has been accused of causing by some critics in the hinterland, legions of smart and energetic individuals continue to be attracted to the city as a place to live, work, and do their part to run (and fix) the system.

Charting a changing demographic

Washington's population grew steadily well into the 20th century, reaching a peak of 802,178 residents in 1950. But as Washington's suburbs grew, the city's population declined, hitting a low of 572,059 in 2000.

The city's racial composition also shifted dramatically in the 20th century. In 1940, roughly 71 percent of residents were White and 28 percent were African American. By 1970, those numbers had flipped: 71 percent of residents were African American and 28 percent were White. Since then, the African American population has declined slightly, while the city has become home to a growing number of Asians and Hispanics.

Recent years have heralded the start of a new trend in Washington's demographics. After decades of decline, the 2010 census revealed that Washington's population had grown 5.2 percent over the decade. Growth has since accelerated, with a 2.7 percent increase measured just between April 2010 and July 2011, making D.C. the fastest-growing "state" in the country. Washington's population growth is on a new trajectory, as Table 1-1 illustrates.

Table 1-1   D.C.'s Population through Two Centuries

Year	Population
1800	8,144
1850	51,687
1900	278,718
1950	802,178
1960	763,956
1970	756,510
1980	638,333
1990	606,900
2000	572,059
2010	601,723

Touting a recession-proof economy

Washington has earned the reputation of a recession-proof city, with plenty of jobs to go around. This relative economic health reflects several factors: increases in the federal workforce, government job security in harsh economic times, and the growth of industry and contractors in the Washington area nurtured by federal spending. Think of it this way: Washington and its environs comprise a very large and successful company town, and the federal government is the company.

Respecting D.C.'s rankings

Best City to Raise Kids. Most Socially Networked City. Second Healthiest City . . . Thanks to its well-educated and high-earning workforce, Washington can be found at the top of numerous city rankings. And the accolades are by no means reserved for Washington, D.C., proper. The 2010 census found that four counties surrounding Washington are among the five wealthiest counties in the country. The top three in the United States (Loudoun and Fairfax in Virginia and Howard in Maryland) are all D.C. suburbs, and they were the only three counties in 2010 with median household incomes above $100,000. Overall, the Washington-Arlington-Alexandria metropolitan area was determined to be the wealthiest in the nation. Even Silicon Valley couldn't beat it. Your tax dollars at work.

Who runs the City of Washington?

Congress is ultimately responsible for governing the District of Columbia as outlined in Article I, Section 8 of the Constitution. Throughout D.C.'s history, Congress has established several forms of governments, both appointed and elected, to run the city's affairs. The current system was set up under the 1973 District of Columbia Home Rule Act. An elected mayor runs the city's day-to-day affairs, while a 13-strong elected Council serves as its legislature. Washington residents also elect the members of 37 Advisory Neighborhood Commissions, which provide input into the local policy-making process. Despite this devolution of responsibility, the city government is restricted from legislating in certain areas (like changing rules on the heights of buildings), and Congress still has the final say on local affairs.

Much to the annoyance of taxpaying D.C. residents, Washington lacks full representation in Congress. The city's license plates rebelliously proclaim "Taxation Without Representation."

Identifying the Washington Establishment

Now that you've taken a whirlwind tour of the city through time and made a quick visit to the city as it exists today, it's time to turn to Washington's most precious resource: its inhabitants. After all, without the people who actually run the federal government and drive the policymaking process, Washington would be only a smallish city with some interesting museums and a handful of Greco-Roman monuments to dead people — in other words, a lot like Europe.

D.C. is clearly much more than that, and its small scale (compared to great political-financial capitals like London and Tokyo) obscures the fact that today Washington exerts enormous influence — arguably greater influence on global politics and business than any other city in the world. To know Washington is not just a matter of knowing one's way from the National Portrait Gallery to the nearest Starbucks. It is essential to understand who lives there and what these people actually do to make the U.S. government work.

You notice quickly upon meeting a few members of the Washington establishment that virtually no one is really "from" Washington. Instead, these people usually come to Washington early in their careers, maybe even for college. Most are not digging for gold, at least as a primary motivation; Wall Street and Silicon Valley offer much better returns for the young and intelligent. They come to D.C. because the work of the U.S. government has its own unique rewards: power and the chance to actually make a difference in the world. Likewise, professionals from the nation's leading banks and law firms may make far less money and squeeze into less luxurious offices when they come to work as staffers at the Department of Treasury or Justice. But the issues they deal with are usually far more interesting and consequential.

Putting the President and Congress in their place

Who are all these people who call Washington home? Not the President or members of Congress. While they are indispensable to the policymaking process, their time in the city is restricted by term limits, constituents, or seemingly inevitable scandal.

True, some members of Congress settle in Washington permanently after they turn in their congressional office keys. (Those who settle permanently *before* leaving office often find that fact comes back to bite at election time.) The real Washington establishment, however, consists of the people under the radar who spend decades there. They hold various titles — federal bureaucrat, lobbyist, lawyer, journalist, consultant, think-tank fellow — but they are alike in being inextricably linked to the policymaking process. They're the ones who make the trains run on time.

Focusing on federal bureaucrats

These are the dark-suited types with the lanyards of security cards. For many of them, the work is not glamorous. Neither is the pay, at least compared to what some could make on Wall Street or in private practice. But the devoted individuals who burrow deep in the bureaucracy and climb their way up the hierarchy can achieve enormous influence and power. J. Edgar Hoover, for instance, became one of the most powerful men in America by turning the FBI into his personal fiefdom. Regulators, to take another example, can hold the attention of entire industries.

Every D.C. operation, from the lowliest agency to the largest department, endeavors to defend and expand its own turf. See Chapter 2 for a thorough introduction to this segment of the D.C. population.

Spotting the lobbyists

At the most basic level, lobbyists strive to influence policy, which is actually what nearly everyone in Washington does (or tries to do). Why else would you want to be in Washington? So, is everyone in Washington a lobbyist? We answer this question in Chapter 3.

Recognizing other voices in the debate

Many other groups and individuals belong to the city's permanent establishment. Among them are think-tank fellows, journalists, long-serving foreign diplomats, activists, and members of NGOs (non-governmental organizations) and international organizations. They may have widely different jobs on paper, but they all, through various means and channels, take part in the policymaking process.

Ironically enough, many of these other voices often define themselves as outsiders in comparison with the insiders who allegedly decide everything behind closed doors. In fact, many of the outsiders are as much a part of the establishment as the insiders they often decry. See Chapter 4 to find out what we mean.

Trying to figure out who really runs the show

Cynics may read the last few paragraphs on the Washington establishment and scoff: "Make Washington work?! These people are the real problem in the political process!" The reason for this disconnect is simple: The workings of Washington can be so inscrutable that it is difficult to understand the purpose of all its moving parts. This book aims to help you gain a greater appreciation for the role of each little gear and spring. It may not turn cynics into true believers; indeed, the cynics may be right on certain points. But at the very least this greater understanding can inform their arguments and sharpen their recommendations for reform.

Ignoring the establishment at your own peril

Most people don't have time for messy politics, regulation battles, or reading the *Federal Register* (the daily journal of the federal government) with their morning coffee. Yet ignoring Washington is risky. You don't have to be a card-carrying conspiracy theorist to acknowledge that the federal government affects our everyday experience.

And yet, Americans vote in far greater numbers in the typical *American Idol* season than in any presidential election. What does that tell us about our democracy? Our government? Americans? (It would seem to tell us that Americans think *American Idol* is a great show.)

Chapter 2

The People behind the Curtain: Federal Bureaucrats

● ●

In This Chapter

▶ Figuring out who fills the ranks

▶ Distinguishing career officials from political appointees

▶ Touring the Executive Office of the President

▶ Filling the federal ranks with Cabinet and department employees

▶ Appreciating the varied missions of federal agencies

▶ Looking the part of a federal employee

● ●

*T*he greater Washington area is home to some 300,000 U.S. federal workers. Once upon a time, the image of federal workers included green eyeshades and trench coats, but these workers — *bureaucrats* — aren't just bean counters. They're an intellectually elite corps drawn from some of the finest schools in the country, and they're largely passionate about their work and committed to do their best. While bureaucrats are often portrayed as mindless drones — and some are exactly that — the truth (as always) is more complicated.

This chapter tells you who these people are, what they do, and how they earn the tax dollars you spend. (Hint: Most of them earn a living by trying to further your interests and the political, economic, and security interests of the United States.)

Embracing the Bureaucracy

Not all bureaucrats are paper pushers. U.S. federal workers may be scientists, medical professionals, economists, mathematicians, negotiators, diplomats, lawyers, officers of the law, military professionals, analysts, and political scientists. Ivy League degrees and six-figure salaries are common in the upper ranks of the career federal service (and even lower-paying jobs offer attractive benefits and are much sought after).

New administrations routinely choose — in addition to some of their partisan supporters — the brightest academics from the best universities, business leaders from the most successful corporations, and financial experts from the top Wall Street firms to serve in significant policymaking agencies such as the Federal Reserve, the Council of Economic Advisers, the Treasury, and the State Department. At least at the top, the so-called revolving door of academics, lawyers, consultants, and other professionals into an administration and back out again is alive and well, and it usually improves both worlds along the way.

Federal workers are entrusted with furthering the interests of the United States domestically and internationally. Their responsibilities include innovative research (medical, aerospace, physics and engineering, food science); intelligence gathering; and sophisticated analysis of threats and opportunities related to politics, security, public health, the economy, and finances.

Federal workers also try to safeguard consumer interests through regulations they draft as part of legislation to be passed by Congress and implemented by regulatory bodies. These workers regard themselves as watchdogs. They draw up regulations that affect Americans' daily lives in many ways; their efforts directly affect how safe your food, water, and medications are, for example. Federal workers also provide policy recommendations to the political leadership in the current administration.

And like the rest of us, they juggle their demanding jobs with the demands of home and family. In their spare time, they coach school sports, run bake sales for their local religious or civic center, pursue hobbies, do home repairs, help their neighbors, raise their kids, and fret about their retirement — just like the rest of America.

Filling Plum Positions: Career Officials versus Appointees

The federal bureaucracy is composed of people who have chosen to pursue a career in government, as well as political appointees who enter government to serve a particular presidential administration. Career officials enter government through competitive means (such as via exams and through open competition for vacancies), while political appointees are selected by the incumbent administration. Appointees usually are selected on the basis of connections with a political party, be it through fundraising, campaign work, previous experience, or a particular political profile. Their role, essentially, is to provide top-down direction with respect to the political and policy priorities of the current president.

The ratio of politically appointed to career officials varies widely by department and agency, and it depends on the seniority and influence of the positions in question. Normally, political appointees are predominant in the higher echelons of an agency, although some federal agencies (such as the CIA and FBI) are staffed almost entirely by career professionals.

The famous Plum Book (nicknamed after its color), officially titled the *United States Government Policy and Supporting Positions,* is closely identified with the system of noncareer appointments. Published after every presidential election, the book contains a list of more than 9,000 jobs that may be filled outside of the government's normal competitive service laws. Most of these positions fall under the executive branch, though a select few posts, such as the Architect of the Capitol and Librarian of Congress, are actually within the legislative branch of government. While all positions may be filled by the President, some require confirmation by the Senate.

Most federal officials do their jobs because they want to make government, and thus our country, work better. But to some extent, how they do their jobs depends on their status as career or appointed officials. If you work with both career officials and political appointees, here are some differences you may notice:

- ✔ Political appointees are more likely to rely on other political appointees when seeking advice or action; career officials are more likely to trust and take advantage of existing bureaucratic structures.

- ✔ Career officials are generally more tolerant of longer time horizons for results; political appointees are very conscious of their limited opportunity to influence events.

- ✔ Career officials run the government. If you want to influence policy formulation, going around or over the head of the responsible career official is a mistake. While in some cases a political appointee may be the official you need to start with, it's always unwise to risk alienating officials whose cooperation you'll need later. (As we discuss later in this chapter, trying to "roll" staffers by going straight to the boss can be disastrous.)

Appreciating the Power of the Executive Office of the President

The Executive Office of the President (EOP) consists of the core White House staff plus several small agencies that are either very political, very powerful, or both. The EOP is headed by the White House Chief of Staff and assists the President in the conception, implementation, and communication of his policies. The EOP includes:

- ✔ The Council of Economic Advisers
- ✔ The Council on Environmental Quality
- ✔ The Executive Residence
- ✔ The National Economic Council
- ✔ The National Security Council/National Security Staff

   ✔ The Office of Administration

   ✔ The Office of Management and Budget

   ✔ The Office of National Drug Control Policy

   ✔ The Office of Science and Technology Policy

   ✔ The Office of the United States Trade Representative

   ✔ The Office of the Vice President

   ✔ The White House Office

The heads of three of these entities — the Council of Economic Advisers, the Office of Management and Budget, and the Office of the United States Trade Representative — are Cabinet rank, as is the White House Chief of Staff. Despite its relatively small size and modest budget, the EOP is the most powerful organization in the federal bureaucracy. Simply put, EOP staffers interpret and communicate the President's wishes to the rest of the government.

While we cover the workings of the White House in greater depth in Chapter 6, many of the institutions that make up the EOP are integral parts of the federal bureaucracy. Some of the more important offices in the EOP include:

   ✔ **The National Security Council (NSC):** The NSC coordinates the development and implementation of the President's national security policy. Chaired by the President, the NSC includes a small group of Cabinet officials supplemented by such key officials as the Director of National Intelligence and the Chairman of the Joint Chiefs of Staff. The President's National Security Advisor is a key participant (and also supervises the work of the National Security Staff, which we discuss in the next bullet).

   The NSC, through the National Security Staff (see the next bullet), manages the formal foreign policy decision-making process in which departments and agencies that have a role in foreign affairs attempt to develop consensus recommendations for the President. We discuss the NSC further in Chapter 7, where we explain the interagency process that helps ensure that federal policy is crafted and implemented with input from all relevant agencies in the executive branch.

✔ **National Security Staff (NSS):** These staffers are some of the hardest-working men and women in the government, routinely working 12 hours or more every day and sacrificing weekends and other personal time to the exigencies and randomness of international affairs. Like other White House personnel, from the President on down, they consider their work critically important to the safety and security of the nation.

The supervisor of the NSS is the National Security Advisor, who can be one of the most important and visible officials in an administration. His (or her) influence is tied directly to his relationship with the President. President Richard Nixon's National Security Advisor, Henry Kissinger, is generally believed to have set the bar on the position, giving orders to the Secretaries of State and Defense.

The highest levels of the NSS are filled by political appointees, usually well-known academics, political figures, or distinguished military officers with long résumés in the national security arena. Midlevel staffers largely come from other agencies — diplomats, military officers, and intelligence professionals who have made a name for themselves and are being rewarded with a chance to work at the center of power. For example, General Colin Powell served as a White House Fellow in the Nixon administration, became National Security Advisor under Ronald Reagan, and later became both chairman of the Joint Chiefs of Staff and Secretary of State.

✔ **The Office of Management and Budget (OMB):** It may have one of the blandest titles in government, but as the administration's official CFO, the OMB exerts enormous influence throughout the federal government. The influence of the OMB director is sometimes called Washington's version of the golden rule: He who has the gold, rules.

When the OMB isn't developing the President's multi-trillion-dollar annual budget request, it's evaluating the effectiveness of the federal government's myriad programs and regulations and developing official administration statements on pending congressional legislation.

✔ **The Council of Economic Advisers (CEA)** and the **National Economic Council (NEC):** Although nearly indistinguishable in name and mission, the CEA and NEC do play somewhat different roles.

   • The CEA, which can be likened to a think tank, was established by Congress in 1946 to advise the President on economic policy and provide him with objective analysis.

   • To demonstrate his seriousness in tackling the country's economic problems, President Bill Clinton created the NEC (which he envisioned as an economic version of the National Security Council) by Executive Order days after his inauguration in 1993. The NEC serves as a policy and interagency coordinator, bringing together the heads of various U.S. departments and EOP offices. It's also an important proving ground for the President's economic team: For example, Robert Rubin, President Clinton's Secretary of the Treasury, started his government service in the NEC.

✔ **The Office of the United States Trade Representative (USTR):** A small but powerful office, the USTR formulates, negotiates, and implements U.S. trade policy. Congress chartered USTR's coordination role in a way that gives the agency a high level of independence from the rest of the federal bureaucracy, making it the premier negotiator of all U.S. trade agreements. USTR also takes the lead in high-profile trade disputes, such as confronting China for stealing intellectual property or challenging the European Union for illegally subsidizing the aircraft industry.

USTR has a statutory mandate to seek the advice of the private sector when formulating trade policy and thus interacts directly with the public more than many other federal agencies.

The U.S. Trade Representative and his or her deputies are all ranked at the ambassador level. One deputy also serves as the U.S. Ambassador to the World Trade Organization based in Geneva.

Running the Nation's Business in the Cabinet and Departments

The Cabinet includes the Vice President and the heads of 15 executive departments: the secretaries of Agriculture, Commerce, Defense, Education, Energy, Health and Human Services, Homeland Security, Housing and Urban Development, Interior, Labor, State, Transportation, Treasury, and Veterans Affairs, as well as the Attorney General, who heads the Department of Justice.

In addition, in every administration a small number of other senior officials are normally accorded Cabinet rank and attend Cabinet meetings as principals. In the Obama administration, these include the White House Chief of Staff, the Administrator of the Environmental Protection Agency, the Director of the Office of Management and Budget, the U.S. Trade Representative, the United States Ambassador to the United Nations, and the Chairman of the Council of Economic Advisers.

The executive departments are the bread and butter of the federal bureaucracy. They employ the majority of federal workers and account for most discretionary spending.

George Washington's administration had only three departments: State, Treasury, and War. Each of these three still exists today, although the War Department became the Department of Defense in the late 1940s. Other departments have been added by Congress as the need arose, and the addition of new executive departments accelerated during the 20th century. The most recently minted organization, the Department of Homeland Security, was established in 2002 in response to the 9/11 attacks of 2001.

All large and complicated organizations have a certain degree of arbitrariness in their structure, and the federal bureaucracy is, for better or worse, no different. Some federal organizations take pride in their diverse composition: the Department of the Interior actually describes itself as the "Department of Everything Else," which is perhaps not a shock considering its daily responsibilities include maintaining our national parks, detecting earthquakes, leasing land for oil drilling, and delivering services to 1.9 million American Indians and Alaska Natives.

Turf battles are another common feature of any bureaucratic landscape, especially when multiple departments are responsible for almost the same issues and when budgetary imbalances curtail or enhance a particular department's influence. Who's really in charge of ensuring domestic safety and security? The Department of Homeland Security would seem the obvious answer, but several national law enforcement agencies, not the least of which is the FBI, are administered by the Department of Justice. And who really drives U.S. foreign policy when, as former Secretary of Defense Robert Gates often said, the Defense Department has more members in its military bands than the State Department has Foreign Service officers?

Each federal agency usually has a core constituency of special interests: The Commerce Department is responsive to the interests of corporate America, and the AFL-CIO is particularly strong in the Department of Labor, for example. The Interior Department's political base of support is in the West, where the big federal land holdings and national parks loom large. And the relationship between the Defense Department and the defense industry was famously described as the "military-industrial complex" in President Dwight D. Eisenhower's farewell address in 1961.

Filling in the Gaps with Agencies from A–Z

In addition to the departments that make up the Cabinet, a rather large number of independent or semi-independent agencies and institutions are also a part of any administration. The exact number depends on how you define a federal agency, but any estimate of the total independent agencies, commissions, government corporations, and other entities would easily reach into the hundreds. Most fall under the executive branch, although a small number are classified as part of the legislative and judicial branches of government.

These institutions fulfill an extremely wide range of missions. For example, they

- Supervise federal elections (Federal Election Commission)
- Regulate the financial industry (Securities and Exchange Commission)

✔ Manage the nation's monetary policy (Federal Reserve System)

✔ Ensure the safety of kids' toys (Consumer Product Safety Commission)

✔ Distribute Social Security checks (Social Security Administration)

✔ Spy on foreign countries (Central Intelligence Agency)

✔ Launch Americans into space (NASA)

✔ Send Americans abroad to serve other nations (Peace Corps)

If you can't find a pattern, that's because one doesn't exist. The federal government itself states merely that independent agencies and corporations "address concerns that go beyond the scope of ordinary legislation" and "are responsible for keeping the government and economy running smoothly." In other words, they can be established by Congress to do pretty much anything.

What to Wear, or How to Spot Federal Workers

The notion that federal workers are conservative, dull, humorless, overpaid, 9-to-5 paper pushers is not true. Well, not usually true. The fact is, most federal workers are dedicated, hardworking, and practically indistinguishable from the rest of Washington's workforce except for their standard uniform of dark suits and ties and the federal security pass looped around the neck or stuffed into a shirt pocket.

Democratic strategist Paul Begala once caustically remarked, "Washington is Hollywood for ugly people." We wouldn't go that far, but federal workers will probably never look as glamorous in real life as the NASA scientists and technicians Hollywood cast for *Apollo 13*. Even in that film America got a taste of the standard federal uniform: white shirts, dark suits, and ties that are just nice enough for an anonymous day at the office (or a funeral) but would look out of place in most of corporate America, where business casual has become de rigueur. In Washington, one rule continues to hold fast: The darker the suit, the more important the official.

Even though some are entrusted with enormous responsibility and influence, federal workers lead relatively normal lives. They don't work in hermetically sealed vaults (or at least most of them don't). They are full-fledged members of the community, and the majority welcome interacting with the private sector and civil society. Ideas are shared over lunch, in coffee shops, in the gym, at PTA meetings, at sporting events, at community cookouts, and on the metro.

In short, except for the hallmark security pass and standard wardrobe, a federal worker is indistinguishable from the rest of Washington — the lobbyists, lawyers, doctors, consultants, teachers, shopkeepers, academics, and the rest.

Commuting in D.C.

Commuter traffic in Washington follows a familiar pattern. If you find yourself standing outside the metro stations at Foggy Bottom, Smithsonian, L'Enfant Plaza, Twinbrook, Medical Center, Federal Triangle, Dupont Circle, Farragut North, or the Pentagon from 7 a.m. onward, you'll see swarms of federal workers on their way to their office, lab, or training station. Stand outside those stations from 5 p.m. onward, and you'll see swarms of them going home. Watch for the *slug lines* — lanes of traffic where an amazingly organized system exists of people in cars (and wanting to qualify for the high-occupancy lanes on the region's highways) picking up people who need rides — and you'll see the ride-share brigade. Brave the traffic jams on the main arteries out of Washington — arteries that back up from 6 a.m. to 10 a.m. and 4 p.m. to 8 p.m. — and watch the early risers and late nighters trudging home, often with a tired toddler from the daycare center. Pull over as the black Navigators roll by with threatening sirens to let senior political figures pass. Being blocked by a motorcade is routine in Washington. Then again, so is seeing the President. (A note of warning: Washington commuters are not good winter drivers, so keep that in mind if you visit Washington from December to February. The ratio of automobile accidents to snowflakes is 2:1.)

Chapter 3

Professional Persuaders: Lobbyists

· ·

In This Chapter

▶ Realizing why citizens can (and should) lobby

▶ Spotting the key interest groups involved in lobbying

▶ Hiring outside lobbying, consulting, or legal firms

▶ Adhering to legislation that regulates the lobbying industry

▶ Utilizing social media

· ·

*A*ttacking lobbyists for their access to "the halls of power" and the influence they peddle has become a requisite talking point for anyone dissatisfied with the ways of Washington. Who are these conspiring, greedy, and apparently just plain awful people, and what role do they play in Washington? Is their entire goal in life to steal from the poor and hurt kittens?

In truth, almost everyone in the United States lobbies in some form or another, either directly (such as by contacting a member of Congress) or through representation by one of thousands of organizations. Why do we all lobby? To advance or protect our interests. But we tend to view our own lobbying efforts very differently from those of paid lobbyists.

In truth, professional lobbyists are (mostly) normal people, many of whom used to be federal workers (who are also mostly normal people; see Chapter 2). They represent all facets of civil society and often inform policymaking debates with expertise and thoughtfulness — two things rarely found in rough-and-tumble media representations of what goes on in Washington. Despite their bad reputation, successful Washington lobbyists know that they are most valuable when they shoot straight and provide solid advice to their clients and to those in government they are trying to persuade. At the end of the day, *what* a lobbyist knows counts more than *who* she knows.

In this chapter, we help you get a handle on why lobbyists exist, what they do, and how they can actually help the political process.

Exercising the Right to Petition

Our Founding Fathers may have thrown British tea overboard, but they decided to keep something else British around: the right to petition. The English Bill of Rights of 1689 affirmed that "it is the right of the subjects to petition the King and all commitments and prosecutions for such petitioning are illegal." Essentially, *lobbying* is exercising the right to petition. And that right is so important to our democracy that our Founding Fathers enshrined the concept in the U.S. Constitution. The First Amendment states:

> *Congress shall make no law respecting an establishment of religion, or prohibiting the free exercise thereof; or abridging the freedom of speech, or of the press; or the right of the people peaceably to assemble, and to petition the Government for a redress of grievances.*

The right to peaceably assemble means that people can gather to discuss their opinions. It also guarantees the right of association in groups, such as political parties, labor unions, and business organizations.

The right of petition means that individuals, acting alone or as part of a group, can freely send criticisms or complaints to government officials. In 1791, when the Bill of Rights was ratified, the American population was small enough that most people could directly petition for a "redress of grievances." But today, with a population of more than 300 million people, direct petitioning is no longer feasible. That's why U.S. citizens need representatives — lobbyists — to petition on their behalf.

The term *lobbyist* was coined during President Ulysses S. Grant's administration (1869–1877) when petitioners for government favor or assistance would assemble in the lobby of the famous Willard Hotel in downtown D.C. in the hope of gaining an audience with members of Grant's inner circle. That image seems quaint now, when lobbying is such huge business and takes place in so many ways. The big business aspect of lobbying is what many people object to; at its height in 2010, it was a $3.5 billion industry employing almost 13,000 registered lobbyists — and that's just reported lobbying at the federal level. Lobbying also takes place at the local, county, state, and international levels.

Identifying Interest Groups

If you aren't convinced that almost everyone in the United States is involved in lobbying, whether directly or indirectly, keep reading. In this section, we focus on the key interest groups with lobbying efforts in Washington, and most likely you have a connection with one or more of them.

Large corporations

We all know that companies lobby. From Goldman Sachs on financial regulatory reform to Microsoft on online piracy laws to Lockheed Martin on defense appropriation, companies exercise their right to petition so they can advance and protect their ability to conduct business and earn profits. In an age when government increasingly makes decisions that affect day-to-day business operations — from food safety standards to the taxes on imported steel — it's no wonder that companies have built up sophisticated lobbying operations to ensure that the government makes decisions that help, rather than hinder, their ability to conduct business and deliver returns to shareholders.

Does corporate lobbying automatically imply greed and selfishness on the part of executives? Far from it. In 1989, celebrated American economist and Nobel Prize winner Milton Friedman made this statement to the National Association of Business Economics regarding an executive's motivations for lobbying:

> A corporate executive who goes to Washington seeking a tariff for his company's product is pursuing his stockholders' self-interest. . . . If he's made a valid, accurate judgment that a tariff will be in the self-interest of his enterprise, he is justified in lobbying for such a tariff.

Why, then, does the public perceive that corporate lobbying is inherently evil? Perhaps because the substantial dollars involved in the lobbying process seem wasteful or smack of bribery. But anyone whose retirement plan includes investments in companies can realize why participating in the federal policy conversation matters to their own bottom line. As shareholders — even very small shareholders — in the nation's corporations, everyone invested in the stock market stands to profit if a corporation takes action that helps it conduct business less expensively and more efficiently.

Who are the biggest guns in the corporate lobbying world? Each year, Congress gives varying degrees of attention to the myriad issues it faces, so examining lobbying spending year by year is sure to result in some anomalies. If a once-in-a-decade bill to regulate your industry is facing a vote in Congress, you'll probably spend extra cash that year to ensure the vote goes the right way. Looking over an extended period of time can reveal who is really engaged in lobbying for the long haul. According to the website Open Secrets (www. opensecrets.org), from 1998 to 2012, these were the top ten corporate spenders for lobbying activities:

- General Electric
- Blue Cross/Blue Shield
- Northrop Grumman
- Exxon Mobil
- Verizon Communications
- Edison Electric Institute
- The Boeing Company
- Lockheed Martin
- AT&T, Inc.
- Southern Company

What do you notice about this list? Despite the vast complexity of the U.S. economy, the top spenders on lobbying are remarkably concentrated in a few industries: three in defense, two in telecommunications, and two electric and natural gas utilities. The others are involved in healthcare, general manufacturing, and oil and gas.

Not surprisingly, these sectors are incredibly dependent on the federal government. If you make fighter jets, your main customer will likely be the federal government. Even if you want to export to foreign markets, you're going to need the federal government's permission. If you are a public utility (such as an electric or natural gas company) or were once a utility (in the case of telecommunications), your industry is, by its very nature of providing a quasi-public service, among the most heavily regulated. Government decisions on new regulations, laws, and procurement can be the difference between making a profit and breaking the bank.

Trade associations

Often companies join together and lobby under the banner of a trade association. Individual companies pool their money and channel their activities through trade associations for various reasons. Forming a trade association is a reliable way to have a louder voice in the debate and to ensure that small entities (for example, individual doctors) who could never fund their own powerful lobbying outfit may — when joined together with thousands or hundreds of thousands of others — wield some influence.

The largest and most powerful trade association is the U.S. Chamber of Commerce. Consistently the top spender on lobbying according to the nonpartisan Center for Responsive Politics, the Chamber is the world's largest business organization, representing the interests of more than 3 million businesses. Chamber members range from mom-and-pop shops and local chambers to leading industry associations and large corporations. Located directly across from the White House, the Chamber goes either head to head or hand in hand with the White House on everything from tax policy to international trade to healthcare reform.

Trade associations may be organized by industry, such as the American Wind Energy Association, the Biotechnology Industry Association, and the National Beer Wholesalers Association, just to name a few. Members of Congress, congressional staff, regulators, and policymakers often consult experts in, or affiliated with, these associations as they deliberate on laws and regulations that would impact the industry in question.

Some critics consider such behavior confirmation of their cynical view of Washington; they see businesses supposedly writing the very same rulebook they are then obligated to follow. But this dialogue is an unavoidable and vital part of the policymaking process. After all, who can expect every member of Congress to know the ins and outs of alternative fuel subsidies, the approval process for biotech drugs, or the arcane set of patchwork laws regulating alcohol in this country? Good trade associations know their industries and the issues they face better than anyone else in Washington.

Trade associations may also be organized by issues. For instance, the International Intellectual Property Alliance (IIPA) is a cross-sector/private sector coalition that strives to improve protection and enforcement of copyrights. IIPA is also representative of another variation of trade associations: an association of associations. In the case of IIPA, it includes seven separate associations representing the publishing, software, film, music, and recording industries.

Here are the top trade associations by expenditures on lobbying activities from 1998 to 2012, according to the website Open Secrets (www.opensecrets.org):

- ✓ U.S. Chamber of Commerce
- ✓ American Medical Association
- ✓ Pharmaceutical Research and Manufacturers of America
- ✓ American Hospital Association
- ✓ National Association of Realtors
- ✓ Business Roundtable
- ✓ National Cable and Telecommunications Association

Not surprisingly, this list affirms that the health industry is among the largest spenders on lobbying activities.

Labor unions

Labor unions are also major lobbyists. From the American Federation of Teachers to the Air Line Pilots Association, labor unions represent — what else? — the interests of their members.

In Washington, laws and regulations are written and rewritten each day that impact workers' benefits and job security. Labor unions ensure that workers' voices are heard when those decisions are being made. For example, one of the largest unions, the American Federation of State, County and Municipal Employees (AFSCME), represents 1.4 million members who work in public service and healthcare. AFSCME represents its members on everything from improving unemployment benefits to raising the minimum wage. Unions represent all sectors of the American workforce.

In instances where a workforce sector isn't represented by a labor union, chances are it still has a lobbying presence. For example, while trial lawyers don't have a labor union of their own, they have a lobbying group representing their interests: the very well-funded American Association for Justice. So do Certified Public Accountants, realtors, and physicians.

Issue-oriented organizations

Passionate about the right to bear arms? The National Rifle Association may be right for you. Concerned about lesbian, gay, bisexual, and transgender equal rights? Check out the Human Rights Campaign. Abortion rights? The National Association for the Repeal of Abortion Laws has you covered. Against abortion? The National Right to Life Committee is in your corner.

Whatever your particular political hot buttons, lobbyists are on your side. Some issue-centered advocacy organizations may consider their work a tad more righteous than the efforts of their corporate counterparts, but truth be told, the fundamental activity they engage in (striving to influence government policymaking) is identical to what the Chambers of Commerce and General Electrics of the world do.

Other interest groups

Don't work for a company, belong to a professional organization, or care about polar bears? An organization is still probably out there lobbying for you. One of the largest and most influential organizations in Washington is AARP, which represents people age 50 and over on prescription drug benefits under Medicare, as well as age discrimination in the workplace.

Who else lobbies? Small towns and big cities, colleges and universities, churches, American Indian tribes, foreign countries . . . the list goes on and on. The breadth and diversity of organizations that lobby in Washington is truly astounding. Some are no more than one-person shoestring operations; others are multimillion-dollar behemoths with palatial offices on K Street. And while the popularity of the issue at hand, or the influence of the organization or lobbyist, often determines who gets heard and who struggles to squeeze past the congressional intern at the door, it's no exaggeration to say that nearly every facet of civil society and the private sector is represented in one form or another.

A quick glance at the potpourri of trade associations and interest groups attests to this fact. Are you a fan of special occasions? Try the Greeting Card Association, and just to cover all your bases, the Envelope Manufacturers Association too. If you're a romantic, you may prefer the National Candle Association. Want to improve America's relations with foreign countries and peoples? Try the British-American Business Council, or (for the more eclectic) the Uyghur American Association. Want to protect your right to enjoy your beverage of choice? Support the American Beverage Association, the Tea Association of the United States of America, or perhaps the Brewers Association. Lobbyists are even represented by the American League of Lobbyists.

Realizing the Role Played by Lobbying and Consulting Firms

Some interest groups lobby on their own; they have in-house staffers who trek up to Capitol Hill and federal agencies to interface directly with decision makers and their staff. Other interest groups outsource; they hire outside experts with

specific issue expertise or with access to particular congressional committees, members, and staff, or to agencies. In fact,
some companies have dozens of firms helping them on any
number of issues. For example, Google has 20 or so firms
lobbying on its behalf on issues as varied as Internet regulation, immigration quotas, and patent reform.

These outside lobbyists are often former members of
Congress, former congressional staff members, or former
political appointees to various agencies. They know how laws
and policy are made, and they know the dynamics behind
who is making them. A 2005 report by the advocacy group
Public Citizen found that since 1998 more than 43 percent of
departing members of Congress have become lobbyists. This
figure counts only those who are eligible: All congressmen
face a one-year ban on federal lobbying immediately after
leaving office. More than half of departing Republicans (52
percent) became lobbyists, while about a third (33 percent)
of departing Democrats did the same. The trend was slightly
stronger among departing senators (50 percent) than departing representatives (42 percent).

In sum, there is no shortage of well-connected lobbyists willing to take up the cause for the right price. This situation can
lead to awkward moments, especially for former elected officials. But many former legislators have proven that voting one
way in Congress has little bearing on the positions they will
advocate for when they join the private sector.

Considering the hundreds of millions of dollars that top corporations and trade associations allocate for lobbying over
the years, it comes as little surprise that the largest lobbying
firms earn tens of millions of dollars annually from their lobbying contracts.

Bringing Legal Firms into the Lobbying Mix

Glance at any listing of the nation's top lobbying firms, and
you'll notice that a number of them are actually law firms.
Why? In Washington, a number of law firms, in addition to
offering the usual legal advice, have lobbyists on hand to help
clients change the law (or keep it from being changed).

If a client has a legal problem, one way of resolving it could involve changing the underlying law or regulation that is causing the problem. Providing clients with this option is just part of giving them the best counsel possible.

Is there really that much difference between advocating for a client in the courtroom and advocating in a federal or congressional office? Instead of solving the legal problem in the judicial system, why not solve it in the executive or legislative branch of government? Lawyers use their knowledge of the law to best serve their clients. Lobbying is a natural extension of this service.

Regulating the Lobbying Industry

In the interest of regulating lobbying activities and promoting transparency, the government has attempted to formulate a definition of the professional lobbyist. But if history is any guide, this effort will need continual refinement. In this section, we explain how the government defines a lobbyist and what current lobbying regulation looks like.

Defining a lobbyist

In 1995, Congress passed the Lobbying Disclosure Act (LDA), which remains on the books today. (It was the first effort to regulate lobbying since 1946; see the sidebar "The 1946 Federal Regulation of Lobbying Act.") According to the LDA, a lobbyist is defined as someone:

- ✔ Who is either employed or retained for financial or other compensation;

- ✔ Whose services include more than one lobbying contact on behalf of the same client or employer;

- ✔ And whose lobbying activities constitute 20 percent or more of his or her working time on behalf of that client or employer during any three-month period.

The 1946 Federal Regulation of Lobbying Act

The federal government's efforts to regulate lobbying date back to the early 1900s, but it was not until 1946 that the first legislation to broadly regulate lobbying activities — the Federal Regulation of Lobbying Act — was passed by Congress. As an effort to enhance transparency, it was largely a failure. For one thing, it ended up covering only individuals who lobbied Congress on federal legislation. Lobbying directed at the executive branch didn't count. Moreover, while lobbyists registered with the Clerk of the House and Secretary of the Senate, the Department of Justice was responsible for ensuring enforcement of the criminal penalties for noncompliance. According to the American Bar Association's *Lobbying Manual,* the lack of communication between the legislative branch and executive branch meant that enforcement left much to be desired. To make matters worse (or better, depending on your point of view), the 1954 Supreme Court decision in *United States v. Harriss* further gutted the legislation of any real effect.

A *lobbying contact* is any oral, written, or electronic communication to a covered official that is made on behalf of a client or employer and relates to certain subjects, which are enumerated in the U.S. Code at 2 U.S.C. §1602(8)(A). These "certain subjects" include the formulation, modification, or adoption of legislation, regulations, executive orders, programs, policies, and positions of the federal government. Communications regarding the execution of a program or policy (like the award of a contract) and the nomination or confirmation of officials by the Senate are also considered lobbying contacts.

Lobbying contacts do *not* include requests for meetings or status reports that don't attempt to influence a legislative or executive official. They also don't include testimony before a congressional panel, information provided in writing at the request of a government official, or communications made in response to government notices requesting comment from the public.

In the definition of a lobbying contact, we use the phrase *covered official.* Covered officials include:

✔ Members of Congress

✔ Congressional staff

✔ The President

✔ The Vice President

✔ Officers and employees of the Executive Office of the President (see Chapter 2)

✔ Any official serving in an Executive Level I position (such as Secretary of State) through an Executive Level V position (such as the Director of the National Park Service in the Department of the Interior)

✔ Any member of the uniformed services serving at grade O-7 or above (meaning a Brigadier General and above in the case of the Army, Marine Corps, and Air Force, and a Rear Admiral, lower half, in the case of the Navy and Coast Guard)

✔ Schedule C Employees (whose positions are listed in *The United States Government Policy and Supporting Positions,* known as the Plum Book; see Chapter 2)

Under LDA, lobbying firms and individual lobbyists must register with the Secretary of the Senate and the Clerk of the House and must file quarterly disclosure reports. Organizations employing in-house lobbyists file a single registration.

Considering the case of foreign agents

Another piece of legislation governing lobbyists is the Foreign Agents Registration Act (FARA). Enacted in 1938, FARA requires persons acting as agents of *foreign principals* (meaning any foreign government, political party, individual, corporation, or other entity) to make periodic public disclosure of their relationship with that principal.

When Congress enacted FARA, it was trying to ensure that the U.S. government and the American people would be informed of the identity of persons engaging in political activities on behalf of foreign principals so that their statements and activities could be put in the context of their associations. The law is administered by the Counterespionage Section in the National Security Division of the United States Department of Justice. (Try saying that three times quickly!)

Diplomats and other official foreign government representatives are excluded from registering per FARA, and an exception exists for anyone engaged in transactions of a solely commercial nature — creating a loophole for people operating in a purely business (nonpolitical) capacity on behalf of a foreign principal.

Until LDA came along, anyone engaged in political lobbying for a foreign individual or corporation was required to register under FARA; today, those people can instead register under LDA. However, anyone who acts as the agent of a foreign government or political party still must continue to register under FARA. Agents must register with the U.S. Department of Justice, disclose detailed financial and business information, and maintain detailed records that are open to public inspection. The definition of an agent under FARA compared with the definition of a lobbyist under LDA is much broader and can include, for instance, work to influence public opinion.

Acting as the agent of foreign powers can be a unique business, partly because your most challenging clients are not your average greedy corporations but, perhaps, blood-stained despots. Yet as with any business, supply will always rise up to meet the demand.

One Washington journalist, Ken Silverstein, decided to test this premise to its logical extreme: With fake business cards in hand, Silverstein approached several Washington lobbying firms to gauge their interest in representing the great nation of Turkmenistan, which, as the State Department notes in its 2010 Human Rights Report, engages in arbitrary arrest and detention, denies due process and fair trial, and engages (reportedly) in torture. Silverstein's phony contract sparked plenty of real interest from lobbying professionals.

But this fiction pales in comparison with some actual lobbying conducted by foreign governments. During the course of his more than two-decades-long career in lobbying and public relations, the late Washington lobbyist Edward von Kloberg III represented such eminent democrats as Iraq's Saddam Hussein, Zaire's Mobuto Sese Seko, and Romania's Nicolae Ceausescu. According to von Kloberg, the only dictator he ever refused was the Somali warlord General Mohammed Farrah Aidid (whose capture was the objective of the 1993 American military operation in Mogadishu that ended tragically and was later chronicled in the book and movie *Black Hawk Down*). Perhaps not surprisingly, von Kloberg fell victim to another journalistic attempt to test the limits of Washington's lobbyists, expressing interest in taking on the case of a phony German neo-Nazi organization.

Following the gifting rules

Members of the House and Senate must follow strict policies regarding lobbying. The most visible of these policies concerns gifts from lobbyists: Members of the House and Senate and their staffs are prohibited from receiving gifts from registered lobbyists and their employers (meaning the clients whose interests they are representing). They may receive gifts from other individuals only if the gift is worth less than $50. Moreover, House and Senate members and their staffs cannot receive gifts totaling more than $100 from one source in one year. Meals, travel, tickets to sporting events, and all physical goods are considered gifts. (Travel is excepted when it is conducted for "fact-finding" trips, meetings, or speeches as related to the duties of members or their staffs.) Keep in mind that both the House and Senate can change their gift rules at any time, so don't be surprised if these numbers change in future Congresses.

In one instance, a lobbyist supposedly was dating a staff member in the office of a U.S. senator, and when it became known that he had given her an expensive diamond ring, he was investigated for violating the $50-limit gift rule. Turns out he had been less than candid about the ring's value; the diamond was fake, and the ring was worth less than $50, so the lobbyist was off the hook with investigators. How he fared with the girlfriend was another matter.

Restrictions and prohibitions are usually preemptive or reactive: preventing something before it happens or trying to prevent it from recurring in the future. Bans on gifts from lobbyists fall into the latter category. Indeed, it was the revelation of truly extravagant and occasionally criminal behavior by some lobbyists, notably Jack Abramoff, that finally compelled Congress to clean up its own house. Before he was a convicted felon, Abramoff was a master of the kind of soft corruption that sends advocates of clean government into apoplectic fits. In one case, Abramoff rented a private jet and arranged a five-day golf outing in St. Andrews, Scotland, for a congressman and several associates. According to prosecutors, this single junket cost a tidy $130,000.

Bribing a public official is a federal crime, often carrying a prison sentence. U.S. bribery laws state that no person may give anything, or offer to give anything, of value "in return for . . . being influenced in the performance of any official act." Under the law, a quid pro quo, including an implied one, must be present for a bribery charge. A campaign contribution can qualify as a "thing of value," as can other services such as meals and massages. The punishment for breaking bribery laws is a prison sentence of up to 15 years and a fine of up to $250,000 (or three times the monetary equivalent of the thing of value, if that amount is greater).

A more vague section of U.S. law that concerns gifts to lawmakers is the *illegal gratuities statute,* which prohibits anyone from offering or giving a public official anything of value "for or because any official act is performed or is to be performed." Unlike a bribe, an illegal gratuity doesn't require a quid pro quo. That is, illegal gratuities can include gifts given as a "thank-you" for an act already taken or an act that may be forthcoming. For instance, if someone gives a lawmaker a fruit basket to say thanks for a vote on a certain appropriations bill, he could be found in violation of the illegal gratuities law, which has a punishment of up to two years imprisonment and a fine of $250,000. While gifts can be given to federal government officials in theory, such gifts can never amount to more than $20 in value ($50 in aggregate in each year) and must not be connected to a specific past, current, or future act.

Lobbying via Social Media

Congressional staffs are mostly populated by young people looking to make their mark in the political arena and, they hope, make a difference. And they communicate a lot differently than their bosses did at their age. Think twice about faxing a press release to staffers in your typical senator's or representative's office; they probably won't read it even if they know what a fax machine is.

Increasingly, congressional offices are using social media to help gather and disseminate information. A survey by the Congressional Management Foundation found that 64 percent of the senior managers and social media managers in congressional offices think Facebook is a somewhat or very important tool for understanding constituents' views and opinions, 42 percent say Twitter is somewhat or very important, and 34 percent say YouTube is somewhat or very important. When it comes to communicating to constituents the views and positions of the senators and congressmen, 74 percent of these same managers think Facebook is somewhat or very important, 51 percent say Twitter is somewhat or very important, and 72 percent think YouTube is somewhat or very important.

Not surprisingly, the survey also showed that the younger the staff member, the more useful social media was considered to be.

Going forward, lobbying efforts will undoubtedly tap into the power of social media. In 2012, for example, the U.S. Department of Agriculture quickly responded to an online campaign that saw tens of thousands of people petitioning for the removal of so-called *pink slime* from the ground beef served in school cafeterias. The days of writing an actual letter to your member of Congress — or even of calling his or her office to express your opinion — may soon be past. You can bet that professional lobbyists are devoting a good chunk of their time and budgets to ensuring that they're utilizing technology to best serve their clients' interests.

Chapter 4

Other Voices in the Debate: Outsiders, Gatecrashers, and Wallflowers

● ●

In This Chapter

▶ Educating and influencing via think tanks

▶ Fighting for a cause with activists and NGOs

▶ Seeing how foreign diplomats work to affect policy

▶ Appreciating the clout of international organizations

▶ Recognizing the substantial power of the media

● ●

*I*f American satirist Ambrose Bierce was right that politics is "a strife of interests masquerading as a contest of principles," certain groups make it their job to sew the masks for the masquerade ball. They are the people who get involved in the policy process because they want the Washington system to produce good policy — when measured by their own standards. Their objective in getting involved in the political arena is not to take control of it but to influence how the various actors in Washington approach an issue that is dear to their hearts.

In a lot of ways, these groups are of a piece with the lobbyists described in Chapter 3 — influencers of a debate rather than deciders. But unlike paid lobbyists, who (along with politicians, staffers, and administration officials) are known as Washington insiders, these groups define themselves as Washington outsiders. In reality, however, many of the outsiders are as much a part of the Washington establishment as the insiders.

In this chapter, we first discuss the four main groups of these outside influencers: think tanks, activists and non-governmental organizations (NGOs), diplomats/foreign governments, and international organizations. Then we examine another vital actor on the Washington stage: journalists and the media, who (usually) maintain the pretense that they exist outside of the political fray when, in fact, they play an enormously influential — and growing — role in Washington policymaking.

Figuring Out What Think Tanks Do

Think tank is an appropriately absurd term for a uniquely Washingtonesque institution. For the uninitiated, the term likely conjures images of a magic thinking box or ideas factory, and that's not too far from the truth.

Trying to influence policy debates

Think tanks are organizations that employ academics, policy wonks, former politicians, retired generals, and the like. These people do research, write policy papers, hold conferences, make speeches, talk on television, and otherwise advance the brand and prestige of their think tanks.

The line between think tanks and academic institutions can be blurry, but these factors tend to differentiate the two:

✔ Think tanks are often established for a particular political purpose, such as advancing the cause of good governance, national security, or liberal or conservative values.

✔ The publications that they issue (such as white papers and policy briefs) are not intended for a cloistered academic audience but for a policymaking audience: the deciders.

The basic purpose of any think tank is to inform the policy debate and serve as a quasi-laboratory for proposals that someday may work their way through the bureaucracy and decision-making echelons (including the legislature) to become actual U.S. government policy.

Think tanks are intrinsic not only to the policymaking process but also to Washington. A University of Pennsylvania study found that the D.C. area has more think tanks than any other city in the world; combined, more than 500 think tanks operate in Washington, Maryland, and Virginia. Not surprisingly, the most influential think tanks are headquartered in the Washington area, and a few well-known institutions that are based elsewhere, such as the Council on Foreign Relations (New York) and Hoover Institution (Stanford University), maintain Washington offices.

Representing a cause or agenda

Like all organizations, think tanks need financial support. Often, they are established by a wealthy and generous bene-factor who wishes to advance a particular cause or political agenda. They use their particular political stance to woo like-minded individuals to contribute to help fill their coffers. (A donation to an influential think tank could give you more bang for your buck in terms of influencing the policy debate than donating to the average candidate for office.)

A quintessential Washington think tank is the Brookings Institution. Founded by philanthropist Robert S. Brookings in 1916 as the Institute for Government Research, it was, according to Brookings, the "first private organization devoted to the fact-based study of national public policy issues." Some think tanks specialize in one issue, while others cultivate a broad field of expertise. Brookings belongs to the latter category and works on a full range of domestic and international issues. Economics, taxes, foreign policy, global development, education, children and families, healthcare — it's as close as a politician gets to a one-stop shop for late-night reading.

While Brookings covers the full spectrum of policy issues and is slightly left of center, other think tanks take a more focused approach. Some think tanks are more closely identified with the conservative end of the policy spectrum, including the Heritage Foundation and American Enterprise Institute. Others, like the Center for American Progress, align more closely with the liberal side of Washington politics. Founded by John Podesta, the Center for American Progress was so closely connected with the presidential campaign of Barack Obama that *TIME* magazine labeled it "Obama's Idea Factory in Washington" soon after his 2008 victory. Not coincidentally, the leader of the Obama presidential transition was the very same Mr. Podesta.

Employing former public servants

Although the term "revolving door" is normally used to describe the practice whereby congressmen and federal workers move back and forth between government and the private sector, it equally applies to former public servants who relocate to one of Washington's think tanks. In fact, think tanks have become a kind of "government in exile" for whichever political party is currently out of power in the White House.

In early 2009, like clockwork, prominent members of the recently departed Bush administration began returning to the think tank world. The Council on Foreign Relations picked up a former Deputy National Security Advisor, Deputy Assistant Secretary of State, and State Department senior advisor. The former administrator of the U.S. Agency for International Development returned to the board of trustees of the Center for Strategic and International Studies. Watch for this pattern to repeat itself during the next transfer of power.

Informing the public

Think tanks can be a valuable tool for the civic-minded reader because they regularly issue a stream of research, analysis, and policy recommendations on all manner of subjects. In keeping with their objective of informing the debate (and spreading their own point of view), most of this material is available on the Internet free of charge.

Unlike the often dry and jargon-laden writing that is commonplace in academics, the writing produced by think tanks tends to be clear, concise, and relevant. After all, their target audience is influential congressional staffers and administration appointees, most of whom have very little spare time in their 16-hour work days. Gaining attention for an idea is the measure of success for the think tank staffer.

Staying up-to-date on what your favorite think tanks are saying about healthcare or national security is an easy way to become more informed about an issue and get ahead of the curve on what may become U.S. government policy in the future.

Analyzing the Efforts of Activists and NGOs

Non-governmental organizations (NGOs) are essentially all entities outside of government, although most definitions usually exclude organizations in the private sector, and sometimes labor too. NGOs often work on a particular issue: saving children in Africa, promoting the rights of a disenfranchised minority, or protecting the environment, for example.

But wait, you say. Haven't we already covered these? Aren't these the same interest groups discussed in Chapter 3 standing shoulder to shoulder with fellow lobbyists from corporations, trade associations, and labor unions? The answer is a complicated and unsatisfying yes and no.

Yes, activists and NGOs are part of the establishment; they lobby the legislative and executive branches of government just like their counterparts on the payroll of the private sector and labor. But unlike these other groups, activists and NGOs typically identify themselves as Washington outsiders, opposed to the insiders. Whereas corporate or labor lobbyists may be happy to admit that they are working to promote the interests of themselves, their members, or their clients, activists and NGOs see themselves as warriors fighting in the defense of their chosen cause célèbre. They don't fight their own fight; they fight the "good fight." They present themselves as white knights in need of a dragon to slay, and more often than not this enemy is found in the corporate lobbying machine.

Yet the relationship between activists/NGOs and corporate lobbyists is more symbiosis than medieval combat. Activists and NGOs exist to promote their policy prescriptions, but fighting corporate influence in Congress and the administration is how and why they thrive and galvanize support.

Corporate lobbyists, needing to justify their own worth to their bosses, can therefore emphasize the threat that activists and NGOs pose to a company's business model or entire industry.

Activists and NGOs have their own time-tested formula to mobilize support for their issues:

1. **Define an issue and take a stand.** This step allows some room for creativity. Worried about oil drilling in Texas? Why not also worry about drilling in Pennsylvania? Concerned about the health effects of smoking? Why not go after soda and fast food too? Activists and NGOs can really take a stand about anything, as long as they justify it as being in the interest of something greater than themselves (in other words, the public good).

2. **Find an enemy and make a claim.** This step also provides room to experiment. Promoting a particular "good" such as good nutrition or environmental conservation would benefit people, but cutting through the daily political chatter to draw attention to an issue is difficult. Creating a fight, particularly a "little guy versus big guy" fight (like in Frank Capra's *Mr. Smith Goes to Washington*) is a tried and tested way of attracting attention.

   So finding an enemy that could be perceived to be threatened by what the activist or NGO is trying to protect or defend is smart advocacy. If the issue is the environmental impact of oil drilling, the enemy is probably the oil companies, and maybe some conniving politicians to boot. If unhealthy foods are the enemy, the activist or NGO is targeting the food and beverage manufacturers and maybe their alliance of big agricultural interests.

3. **Create a message to rally support to the cause.** An objective analysis, complete with PowerPoints, of the possible impact of oil drilling on the local caribou population probably won't do. The activist or NGO needs

to grab people's attention. Think *Silent Spring* — or, for you younger folks, the movie *Super Size Me*. The goal isn't to exaggerate, just extrapolate:

> "At this rate every child in America will be overweight by 2020."

> "If glacial melting continues to accelerate, Manhattan Island will be under 3 feet of water by 2050."

Will this actually happen? Who knows, but parents and New Yorkers will sure take notice.

Without the activism of the past, we might still be toiling 15-hour days in dangerous workplace conditions, only to come home to firetrap apartments where we might get sick dining on potentially unsanitary food. Most Americans would agree that government regulation has seriously improved our lot by reducing the risks we face in our daily lives. Then, as now, special interests argued that such regulation is ineffectual, burdensome, and sometimes even counterproductive. But for activists and NGOs, it's one victory down and on to the next battle.

Feeling the Influence of Foreign Governments

Washington may be the capital of the United States, but drive around Washington and you're more likely than not to see a foreign flag before you see the Stars and Stripes wafting in the breeze. Embassies of more than 175 foreign states are located in the district, many concentrated in a ritzy section of Massachusetts Avenue known as Embassy Row.

Foreign embassies are Washington institutions. Politicians, corporations, and interest groups come and go, but in a hundred years' time it's likely that the list of foreign countries with a diplomatic presence in the capital will closely resemble today's. Some diplomats have stayed so long that they have become institutions themselves: Prince Bandar bin Sultan,

Saudi ambassador to the United States from 1983 to 2005, was a notably close friend of the Bush family. Singaporean ambassador Chan Heng Chee has been in Washington since 1996, making her one of the longest-serving female envoys to Washington. Of course, time spent in Washington does not automatically make one a member of the permanent establishment. Taking part in the policymaking process is also a prerequisite.

Foreign governments, often through their diplomatic representation in Washington, are integral participants in the U.S. policymaking process. Take away their diplomatic immunity, and they are a special interest lobbyist like all the rest. And just like special interests, their effectiveness is measured in the weight of their voice, the persuasiveness of their arguments, and the degree of their access.

Like other lobbyists, some foreign governments are more successful than others. Among the most successful participants in this game of international lobbying was William Wiseman, a British intelligence officer stationed in the United States during World War I. Wiseman became a close associate of President Woodrow Wilson and his chief advisor Colonel Edward House. (Wiseman even vacationed with the President in the summer of 1918.) One British observer commented that Wiseman was "the only person, English or American, who had access at any time to the President or Colonel House."

Needless to say, most foreign officials never get more than a handshake from the U.S. commander-in-chief. But like other special interests, their success depends on how many doors they can open and whom they can persuade to do what they want.

Foreign diplomats use the same tactics that other lobbyists employ. They engage with both the executive and legislative branches, occasionally even playing one against the other to get their way. They cultivate supporters in government and Congress whom they can rely on to argue their case with the American public and with any intransigent colleagues. Understanding the intricacies of the Washington system makes such diplomats valuable inside their own governments, too. Moreover, foreign diplomats who cultivate relationships with congressional staffers and administration officials can help improve U.S. relations with their home country over time, because the personal connections they make can be drawn on as such people achieve higher office.

Diplomats also leverage outside groups, like expatriate networks or bilateral business councils, to reinforce their mes-
saging. Foreign governments have other tools, like cultural
promotion or organized trade missions, to vary their tactics.
A lot of coordination exists among embassies of different
countries that happen to have common interests in U.S.
policy. Many of them employ professional lobbyists, as we
note in the previous chapter.

Of course, foreign governments are not identical to the special interest lobbyists that represent corporations and labor
unions. Foreign officials don't have to register as lobbyists
or report on all their activities and meetings with covered
officials. But they also have to battle to be heard: While
big domestic special interests may represent thousands of
American workers or icons of American industry, few foreign
officials can draw a direct link between their interests and
a congressman's constituents or reelection prospects. The
result is that many diplomats spend most of their time just
trying to get attention. And unlike special interests, they normally can't flee town when they get unwanted attention.

Interacting with International Organizations

International organizations are institutions that exist among
or above national governments. They are established to
address transnational problems and facilitate intergovern-
mental cooperation on issues that require a multilateral
approach. To the chagrin of isolationists, and to the horror of
conspiracy theorists, international organizations can sometimes take on degrees of supranational authority. Think of
the U.N. Security Council authorizing military action against
Iraq (that would be the first Gulf War) or the World Trade
Organization finding a country's trade policy noncompliant
with global trade rules.

This latter case is a good example of how international organizations play a policymaking role in Washington. Quite literally,
they can compel the U.S. government to adjust its policies
when those policies are found to be inconsistent with the obligations the United States has pledged to uphold. Washington

politicians may not always accept outside advice with open arms, but as the world becomes more interconnected, and sovereignty becomes less rigid, outside organizations will inevitably play a greater role in Washington decision-making.

The very nature of international organizations means that the U.S. government is often a stakeholder in them and can leverage them for its own purposes, which makes them unlike other operators in Washington. In the 1990s, for example, the International Monetary Fund (IMF), which often serves as a lender of last resort for countries suffering from acute budget deficits or plummeting foreign reserves, demanded that countries receiving its loans implement a series of economic reforms known as the "Washington Consensus." These policy recommendations, which included trade liberalization, privatization, and deregulation, closely mirrored the economic policy prescription that U.S. officials had advocated with foreign governments. Having a third party convey such a message is useful for Washington, especially because the United States is still looked upon suspiciously in certain corners of the world.

Sometimes the United States takes a more direct and forceful approach. For example, determined to increase pressure on Argentina to start living up to its international obligations and repay billions in debt to creditor nations (like America) and bondholders, in September 2011 the Obama administration announced that it would use its voting share in the Inter-American Development Bank and World Bank to vote "No" on all new lending to Argentina. In this case, an international organization literally expanded the options available to U.S. policymakers to tackle this issue.

The federal government is one of the largest funders of international organizations, which often rely on a few rich country members to finance their activities. In fact, the reason poor countries are often very active in international organizations is that their participation (their airfare, hotel, and board) is paid for by the organization, and thus ultimately, the U.S. taxpayer.

This dependence on the largesse of Washington can backfire for organizations that cannot read U.S. politics. In late 2011, for example, the U.N. Educational, Scientific and Cultural Organization (UNESCO) voted to admit Palestine as its newest member, even though the Obama administration loudly warned that U.S. law prohibited it from funding U.N. agencies that recognize Palestine as a state. The administration wasn't bluffing: A scheduled payment of $60 million was immediately put on hold, and UNESCO faced the very real potential that 22 percent of its annual budget would disappear.

All Press Is Good Press: The Media

Press in Washington is unavoidable. The White House Press Corps hounds the President's every move, gaffe, and sneeze. Their counterparts do the same on Capitol Hill, although with 535 members of Congress to chase, sometimes oddball behavior and career-ending scandals escape notice longer than they should. Here, we explain who we're referring to when we talk about *the media,* how these entities operate, and the reasons they wield increasing power in Washington policy debates.

Spotting the many players

The Washington press can be divided into a number of different categories, which we cover in this section.

National, local, and foreign media outlets

National media and many foreign media outlets have requisite Washington bureaus. The former includes *The New York Times* and *The Wall Street Journal,* both of which regularly break major Washington stories. For many years, big city newspapers across America also maintained a presence in the capital, although in recent years budget shortfalls have forced many of these outlets to shut their Washington bureaus.

Of course, Washington also has its own local media market. *The Washington Post* is the major local paper, and because local news is national news (remember that "local" break-in at the Watergate?), it competes with the *Times* and *Journal* for a national audience. Since 1982, it has also competed with *The Washington Times,* a conservative paper that was a favorite of Ronald Reagan's but has never succeeded in approaching the *Post*'s number of subscribers.

Members of the foreign press often show up at committee hearings, conferences, and think-tank talks related to their country of origin, but as a rule they don't enjoy the same access offered to national media and are far less likely to get any Washington scoops. Here are some of the foreign media outlets that wield the most influence in Washington:

- ✔ **The *Financial Times* and *The Economist*:** These British publications are required reading in official Washington, and (unlike most foreign media outlets) each regularly scoops the American news media on important political and financial stories.

- ✔ **BBC America:** This TV network is widely watched not just in Washington but throughout the United States.

- ✔ **Al Jazeera:** An independent broadcast network head-quartered in Qatar, Al Jazeera provides Americans with alternative views on important and controversial Middle Eastern developments and also covers America for Middle Eastern audiences through that prism.

- ✔ **RT (Russia Today):** Owned by the Russian government company RIA Novosti, this TV network has more recently entered the market by broadcasting in English in the United States with its own alternative take on U.S. politics.

Specialist media outlets

The capital is also host to a diverse array of specialist media outlets. Several of these, including the *National Journal, Congressional Quarterly, The Hill,* and *Roll Call,* conduct in-depth reporting on the federal government and Congress in particular. In recent years, *Politico* has attempted to imitate this intense political focus while appealing to a broader audience on the web and across the country.

Even these papers are pretty broad-based in comparison to extremely issue- and industry-specific publications. Companies like BNA (now owned by Bloomberg) have teams of reporters that cover federal activities in narrow silos like the environment, healthcare, homeland security, and trade. They then charge hefty fees to corporate clients who need to stay abreast of the issues — and who know that such specialized intelligence will appear too late, if ever, in more mainstream media outlets.

24-hour outlets: Cable news and social media

The newest players on the block are the 24-hour cable news channels and social media. Most Americans are probably all too familiar with the major U.S. cable news networks. CNN, Fox News, and MSNBC cover the national political scene with less depth than the major national papers but greater urgency than an emergency room doctor. In fact, in the eyes of some, the "He said/She said" interminable political back-and-forth that these networks have fostered has seriously influenced the political tone in Washington.

The cable news channels have been joined by an even more unfiltered, 24/7 media player that is collectively referred to as *social media.* At the upper end of this spectrum are professionally run news sites that aggregate news stories and blog postings. At the lower, more scattered end of the spectrum is everything from Facebook pages and Twitter tweets to YouTube videos and personal rants.

Breaking news in a cutthroat environment

How do the media actually operate? What are their motivations and limitations? For starters, most (though certainly not all) media companies are for-profit enterprises, and as classifieds and subscription revenues are drying up, advertising is king. At the same time, the Internet has eliminated some of the considerable costs that traditionally were associated with reporting politics in a meaningful way, increasing the range of sources available to people who want news and analysis. (The hometown paper and national syndicates aren't the only options anymore.)

In practice, this means that media outlets face ever-increasing pressure to gain attention from more viewers and readers: The more eyeballs on the website or the more tablet app downloads, the better. The fastest way to attract attention in a sea of wire reports and nonstop talking heads is to break news. This fact has led to two emerging trends in the media landscape:

  ✔ **Political spin machines:** Political PR and rumor-mongering are nothing new, but they are increasingly reaching new levels of sophistication. From coordinated campaigns of talking heads armed with identical talking points, to faux grass-root movements *(astroturfing),* to "independent" third-party advertisers (who introduced *swiftboating* to the American political lexicon), political spin machines are designed to make news and, in the best cases, write journalists' stories for them.

✔ **Citizen journalism:** This term is a catchall for journalistic activities carried out by nonprofessionals. What it means is that in the era of camera-equipped smartphones in every pocket, no public figure can ever assume he or she is not being recorded. Not surprisingly, human behavior has not adapted quickly enough to 21st-century technologies, as an increasing number of gaffes and mini-scandals attest.

Citizen journalism, made possible by the Internet, has not only increased the exposure public officials face on a daily basis, but it has also broken down the few remaining barriers imposed between the powerful and their constituents. Any hint of a scandal, which the media might once have sat on for ethical reasons ("We need to cross-check this") or legal reasons ("We might get sued for this"), can now be leaked through innumerable amateur and semi-professional political blogs and websites.

Because the media now includes a vast concatenation of bloggers, Tweeters, YouTube posters, and Facebook members, the vast majority of whom have no journalistic training, it has become nearly impossible to determine which stories are accurate (meaning they've been multiply sourced and confirmed by journalists trained in the profession) and which are rumors or deliberate falsehoods initiated by amateurs with an axe to grind. And because, as Mark Twain allegedly said, "A lie travels halfway around the world before the truth can get its pants on," the public's confidence in the journalistic trade has seriously eroded.

However, politicians are not always helpless victims in this fully exposed, barrier-free world. In fact, they are often willing participants, boasting on their Facebook pages and tweeting as if it were the neatest thing since party lines. This latest form of political ridiculousness has, in a few short years, expanded our lexicon (thank Sarah Palin for inventing the term *refudiate*) and given us another reason never to go into the congressional gym (thanks to former Representative Anthony Weiner).

Influencing policy (for better or worse)

The media — and here we are speaking both of actual journalists and the general medium of communication — are an integral part of Washington politics and, by extension, the policymaking process. Politicians can rise or fall because of a single tweet. Policies are exalted or pilloried according to who wrests control of the media narrative.

Some critics have accused the mere existence of the media with altering the political debate. The 24-hour news cycle, they say, has turned every little decision into a breaking news story and has, in turn, encouraged politicians to use every vote as a test of brinkmanship and showmanship. In this analysis, all the blogs, web portals, and influencers reacting to events in real time on services like Twitter are making politics a nonstop cacophonous conversation, polarized around party lines, where the object is not to increase public understanding but to win a perceived advantage over one's political opponents.

But the changing media landscape in Washington has also introduced what would generally be considered positive aspects to the policymaking process. The spread of information rapidly and cheaply means that any voter who has the time and motivation can educate himself about the actions of the federal government like never before — and he can just as easily express himself should he have something to say. Also, organizing among geographically or demographically disparate groups of individuals has never been easier, allowing grass-root movements to grow literally overnight. Many Americans who previously felt alienated from politics find it easier than ever before to express their opinions, associate with likeminded strangers, and generate pressure for their preferred changes to public policy.

Chapter 5

Congress

● ●

In This Chapter

▶ Reading Congress's job description

▶ Eyeing the structure and leadership of the Senate and House

▶ Figuring out why Congress works by committee

▶ Tracing the path from bill to law

▶ Following the money trail

● ●

Congress occupies the U.S. Capitol: a massive, stunning white structure with a famous dome that sits at the end of the Mall in Washington, D.C. (on a hill — hence Capitol Hill, or simply *The Hill*). From the halls of Congress, bills are born, expanded, contracted, and then sent to the President's desk for signature. From these same halls, a legislative chain of checks and balances is forged that aims to help ensure the proper functioning of the executive and judicial branches of government. Currently, 535 members, who represent all 50 states, work within Congress's two chambers: the Senate and the House of Representatives.

In this chapter, we lay out the functions of Congress, how these functions structure the way legislators conduct the business of the nation, how the members of Congress come to find themselves walking the Capitol's hallowed halls, and what they do in order to stay there.

Browsing the Basic Responsibilities of Congress

At its core, Congress exists to prevent the executive branch from exercising total control over U.S. legislation — something the writers of the Constitution wished to avoid at all costs lest the United States become just another monarchy or dictatorship. In this section, we explain the work Congress does to achieve this end.

With Congress possessing the sole power to draft and pass the laws of the land — leaving the President limited to signing or vetoing said laws — no one group can hold sway over the direction in which the United States is governed. (Even when a single party controls the executive branch and both the Senate and House, that party's competitors still have a say in how Congress acts.) While Congress is often seen as a group that slows rather than expedites the process of democracy, its function as a body of debate and compromise is essential to the health of the American experiment.

Wielding the power of the purse

First and foremost, the work of Congress is about money — a subject that, one way or another, touches the daily lives of every American citizen.

Members of Congress determine how much, how often, and in what circumstances to tax the American people. They also decide how tax revenues are appropriated and spent across the entire federal government. (Most of your tax money is actually spent by the executive branch, although Congress and the federal courts also have their own budgets.) Commonly referred to as *the power of the purse,* this responsibility is the primary check on the executive branch's power. In other words, this function of Congress prevents the President from ever using the national treasury as his personal bank account.

Though both the Senate and House have equal authority, only the House is authorized to originate revenue and appropriations bills. (And, as we explain later in this chapter, the House is more beholden to popular opinion than the Senate because of its structure.)

Overseeing the executive branch

Another check on the executive branch is *congressional oversight:* the power to investigate and oversee the executive branch, usually carried out by congressional committees. (We discuss congressional oversight again in Chapter 7 when explaining the checks and balances that ensure federal policy is being properly implemented.)

The Senate plays a particularly important role in checking the power of the executive branch because it has the power to confirm Cabinet officials, judges, and other high officials — a form of leverage that senators often exploit until they get what they want from the President. In addition, the Senate has the power to approve — to "advise and consent" as the Constitution puts it — all treaties that are negotiated by the executive branch. (President Richard Nixon once remarked that in his dealings with the Senate he got a lot more advice than consent.)

Carrying out other constitutional duties

Congress has many additional powers within its grasp, including some that are crucial to national defense. As laid out by Article I, Section 8 of the Constitution, its powers include:

- ✔ Borrowing money from other nations

- ✔ Declaring war on other nations

- ✔ Determining and establishing the structure of the military (and doling out money for national defense)

- ✔ Establishing federal laws that don't interfere with the rights of individual states to govern their own populations internally

This last power is often a sticking point between the competing political parties, who make up the overwhelming majority of Congress's members and often espouse different views about how much the federal government should poke its nose into issues that states usually handle themselves. But pay close attention: Political arguments masquerading as defenses of states' rights are not always telling the whole story. (Remember slavery?) Politicians from all sides have used this argument when convenient and quietly dropped it when not.

Studying the Structure of Congress

In this section, we outline the structures of the Senate and House so you can see who's representing the states, how often you elect members of Congress, and how long they serve. We then list the leadership positions in each chamber so you can see who wields the most power on Capitol Hill.

Spotlighting the Senate

The Senate is composed of two elected officials from each state in the Union, so the Senate has 100 members. In the Senate, each state gets an equal vote: Wyoming and California each have two representatives, as do Alaska and New York. Equal representation in the Senate was an essential component of the Great Compromise of the Constitutional Convention (back in 1787), reassuring smaller states that their voices would not be drowned out by the more populous ones.

Senators serve six-year terms, and Senate races are staggered so this body doesn't experience radical turnover in any given election year; one-third of Senate seats are up for election every two years. (Historical tidbit: Initially, senators weren't elected, but rather appointed by state legislatures.) Someone has to be at least 30 years old to run for a Senate seat.

The Senate is considered a higher chamber than the House; the Senate is the *upper house* of Congress. That does not mean that it's more powerful than the House; in fact, because the Senate cannot introduce revenue and appropriations bills, you can argue that the House has more power. However, as we note in the preceding section, the Senate has greater oversight over the executive branch than the House does because it can approve or reject nominations and treaties.

Homing in on the House

The House of Representatives has 435 members, each of whom serves only a two-year term. Someone must be at least 25 years old to run for a House seat.

The entire House goes up for election every two years, which means it can experience much more significant turnover in any given election than the Senate can. This fact should help to ensure that power doesn't become entrenched within the chamber; voters have a regular opportunity to elect people who will most fully and accurately represent their interests in Congress. (Of course, this ideal is not always achieved. In the upcoming section "Investigating the Importance of Money," we discuss campaign financing and how it affects legislators' tenures and actions.)

The Constitution made sure that each state has at least one representative in the House, but not all states are represented equally (as they are in the Senate). Instead, the number of House seats in a state is determined by its population, thus giving greater representation to states with greater populations. (Wyoming has 1 representative; California has 53. Alaska has 1 representative; New York has 29.) This was the other major component of the Great Compromise of 1787 and, naturally, was favored by the larger states.

The Constitution did not specifically state that the House should have a total of 435 members. In 1911, after seeing the House grow many times in the early years of the republic, Congress fixed the number at 435.

The House is technically the *lower house* of Congress, and it's considered the legislative body of the people — representing the actual population of the United States and, at least in theory, responding more readily than the Senate to the population's will.

Spotting the legislative leaders

Two of the most prominent members of Congress are the President of the Senate and the Speaker of the House. The Senate president's seat is filled by the nation's Vice President. The Speaker of the House is a representative within the House's majority party who is elected by other representatives on the first day of a new Congress. (The Speaker could, by law, be a member of the minority party, but that doesn't happen in practice.) Both figures preside over the debates and votes within each chamber and can serve as a tie-breaking vote should it become necessary. Along the chain of succession, the Speaker of the House is third in line behind the President and Vice President.

Other bigwigs in the Senate include:

- ✔ **President Pro Tempore:** Elected by other senators, this person — who is normally the longest-serving senator from the majority party — presides over sessions when the Vice President is absent.

- ✔ **Senate Majority Leader:** Elected by other senators, this member of the majority party sets the general positions of the party related to legislation being drafted and debated.

- ✔ **Assistant Majority Leader:** Known as the *Majority Whip,* this senator is responsible for rounding up votes.

- ✔ **Senate Minority Leader:** Elected by other senators, this member of the minority party sets the general positions of the party related to legislation being drafted and debated.

- ✔ **Assistant Minority Leader:** Known as the *Minority Whip,* this senator is responsible for rounding up votes.

- ✔ **Secretary of the Democratic Conference:** This Democratic senator is responsible for recording minutes during party meetings or caucuses.

- ✔ **Secretary of the Republican Conference:** This Republican senator is responsible for recording minutes during party meetings or caucuses.

In the House, the other power positions are:

- ✔ **House Majority Leader:** This representative is responsible for daily management of the House floor, although his or her power depends upon the Speaker.

- ✔ **House Minority Leader:** This leader of the minority party in the House is waiting for his or her turn to become Speaker.

- ✔ **House Majority Whip:** This person is responsible for managing the legislation the majority party has proposed and for corralling the majority party members.

- ✔ **House Minority Whip:** This person is responsible for managing the legislation the minority party has proposed and for keeping the members of that party in line.

Whichever political party holds a majority among the members of either chamber has a great deal of power, from choosing majority leaders who can help set a congressional agenda, to holding the senior positions within congressional committees. The majority party can wield a great deal of influence over the business of Congress, most visibly in the passage or rejection of bills whose contents cause members to vote along party lines.

Appreciating the Committee Process

Both the Senate and House of Representatives are structured by committee. Congressional committees are charged with gathering information, evaluating the options on certain issues, and proposing solutions for the full Senate or House to consider.

To be blunt, no member of either chamber could possibly learn enough about every subject under consideration to make educated decisions about how to vote. Many (well, at least some) of these folks are really smart, but they may vote on a *lot* of complex legislation in any given session. That's why the committee structure, which we explain in this section, exists.

Helping legislators gain expertise

In committees, members of Congress can focus on particular subjects that they care about or have experience with. The choice of who sits on a particular committee is most often based on its importance to the legislator's constituents or region, or on that person's own background. In time, the committee process allows members to become subject matter experts and, in turn, empowers them to advise the entire Congress on that particular subject.

A committee learns about the topic of certain legislation through public hearings, during meetings with stakeholders and professional lobbyists, and courtesy of mandated research entities responsible for providing nonpartisan information to members. For example, the Congressional Budget Office (CBO) is responsible for providing economic data and analysis to members of Congress. And the Congressional

Research Service (CRS) publishes reports on issues in order
to provide ideas for legislation or help members analyze a
certain issue. (The CRS also consults on procedures and helps
resolve discrepancies that may arise between the House and
the Senate.)

Serving as a source of power

Each committee appoints a head from the majority party and
a senior ranking member from the minority party. A hierarchy
often emerges among the committees, especially depending
on what particular interests a lawmaker has with regard to
his or her constituencies, political aspirations, lobbying influences, fundraising influences, and personal passions. A senior
or ranking position within a powerful committee is a quick
way for a congressperson to stand out and make a mark on
the legislative agenda of the congressional session.

Senate committees

The Senate has 16 standing committees, as well as select committees,
special committees, joint committees, and — just for good measure —
subcommittees that support the work
of the main committees. The standing
committee names offer a pretty clear
indication of their areas of legislative
influence:

- Agriculture, Nutrition, and Forestry
- Appropriations
- Armed Services
- Banking, Housing, and Urban Affairs
- Budget
- Commerce, Science, and Transportation
- Energy and Natural Resources
- Environment and Public Works
- Finance
- Foreign Relations
- Health, Education, Labor, and Pensions
- Homeland Security and Governmental Affairs
- Judiciary
- Rules and Administration
- Small Business and Entrepreneurship
- Veterans' Affairs

House committees

The House has 20 standing committees, as well as a Permanent Select Committee on Intelligence. (A *select* committee is established to do special work that isn't covered by a standing committee.) Most of the standing committees, which are listed here, are divided into subcommittees to create quite an intricate web.

✔ Agriculture

✔ Appropriations

✔ Armed Services

✔ Budget

✔ Education and Labor

✔ Energy and Commerce

✔ Ethics

✔ Financial Services

✔ Foreign Affairs

✔ Homeland Security

✔ House Administration

✔ Judiciary

✔ Natural Resources

✔ Oversight and Government Reform

✔ Rules

✔ Science, Space, and Technology

✔ Small Business

✔ Transportation and Infrastructure

✔ Veterans' Affairs

✔ Ways and Means

Committees have a lot of power, including the power to write legislation. Therefore, they are a means for individual members of Congress to build seniority, as well as personal power and influence. While certain procedures exist for bypassing committee input and directly introducing bills on the House floor, these procedures are very difficult to carry out, making committees the preferred conduit for advancing legislation.

Another function of congressional committees is to carry out the power of oversight, monitoring and investigating the agencies of the executive branch. We explain this function in detail in Chapter 7.

Bringing a Bill — and Possibly a Law — to Life

The path of a bill from its introduction in one of the congressional chambers to its arrival on the President's desk can seem byzantine to an outsider. If you're old enough to have ever watched the scene in *Mr. Smith Goes to Washington* where Jean Arthur explains how it all works to Jimmy Stewart, this section may be a bit redundant; but don't worry, we can be just as charming as Jean Arthur. (In case you don't know, Jean Arthur was the Reese Witherspoon of her day.)

A bill can originate in either chamber of Congress (except for a revenue or appropriations bill, which must originate in the House). For the bill to reach the President's desk, however, it must be passed by both houses.

The life of a bill starts with legislation written (usually) by one or several senators or representatives. The legislation is sent to the appropriate committee, where committee members debate and potentially redraft it. Throughout this process, congressional staff members, who are often experts in the subject matter at hand, play a critical role.

After the bill clears the committee, it's put in the docket for all members to debate it on the floor of the chamber where it originated. More amendments and changes are made, and eventually, a vote is called.

For the bill to pass in the House, a simple majority of at least 51 percent of all members must vote "Aye." (By this measure, the House's current makeup requires 221 members voting in favor of a bill to ensure passage.) In today's Senate, a three-fifths majority (60 votes) is often needed to end debate and move to a vote; actual passage requires only a simple majority of "Aye" votes. Obviously, a bill has a tougher time moving through the higher chamber, which allows the Senate to provide a check and balance against the more rough-and-tumble House.

The bill then moves to the other chamber of Congress, where it may be changed or amended again. However, for executive approval, both chambers must pass identical versions of the bill. A sort of legislative ping-pong can start, should the Senate wish to change a House-generated bill or vice versa. The back-and-forth can be frustrating and exhausting, but without the process of compromise, one chamber, one party, or even one individual could wield unchecked power.

If you get the feeling that we're racing through the process in this section, you're right. That's because we devote more real estate to this discussion in Chapter 7 about policymaking. The reality is that lots of players, both inside and outside government, influence how a bill is written, rewritten, and amended. And lots of players influence how legislators vote on a given bill. For us to pretend that the bill-to-law process involves only senators, representatives, and (finally) the President would be misleading, so we offer the larger, more accurate picture of the process in Chapter 7.

Capitol life

The U.S Capitol Complex is a major city employer, architectural landmark, tourist destination, and historical site. Most people recognize the U.S. Capitol because of its distinctive dome, but the daily legislative work is conducted in the nearby House and Senate office buildings, which are connected by a labyrinth of subterranean tunnels. There's even a small subway system!

As in any organization, office space denotes power. Senators enjoy nicer offices than their counterparts in the House. Veteran legislators with high-profile committee positions usually have larger and more luxurious quarters than the rank and file. Outgoing members are literally moved to the basement (officially the *Departing Member Services Center*). Watch out: Legend holds that a Demon Cat roams the lower reaches of the Capitol at night, sightings of which portend national tragedies or presidential transitions.

Staffers in member offices and on committees do the bulk of the actual work in Congress, especially because members are often back in their home districts or out fundraising. Competition for these jobs is fierce, space is limited, and pay is relatively low. Job security is also wanting. But there are few easier ways for ambitious individuals to take part in the high-level policymaking process at an early age, and experience working on the Hill can be generously rewarded in the private sector.

Investigating the Importance of Money

Money may wield more influence than any one person or ideological system in shaping the congressional agenda. Winning candidates for the House spent on average $1.4 million in the 2010 elections, according to the Center for Responsive Politics, while the winning Senate candidates spent on average a whopping $9.8 million.

Not only does it cost a great deal to launch a successful campaign, but also the promise of more money down the road for future campaigns can help guide a legislator's hand toward an "Aye" or "Nay" vote. You may not like to hear it, but that's the truth, and the legislative power of money is the topic of this section.

Focusing on campaign fundraising

Congressional election law is administered by the Federal Election Commission (FEC), which seeks to ensure that money is spent ethically and fairly across campaigns. Of course, it doesn't always work out like that, but certain practices do help to level the playing field.

The two major political parties each have a national committee whose goals are to gain or maintain power in both the legislative and executive branches of government. These committees raise money and distribute it to favored candidates in elections across the country during each cycle. The FEC limits the amount of money each campaign can receive from the Democratic or Republican national committee. (For 2011–2012, the limit is $5,000 per election except for Senate races; a special, inflation-indexed limit of $43,100 is set for each Senate campaign.)

An individual donor is restricted to giving a maximum of $2,500 per congressional or presidential candidate. However, that same person can donate more than 12 times as much to a political party's national committee. Therefore, if someone is looking to influence an upcoming election, an indirect donation (to the committee instead of the campaign) can have much greater influence. National campaign committees, however, make the final decisions on where those dollars are spent.

Playing with PACs and special interests

The campaign finance game changed dramatically in 2010, when the U.S. Supreme Court, in the case *Citizens United v. Federal Election Commission,* decided that the First Amendment to the U.S. Constitution allows the expenditure of money as a form of free speech. This ruling lets independent organizations called Political Action Committees (PACs), which are "uncoordinated" with an election campaign, raise and spend as much money as they want on behalf of the candidate of their choice. As a result, major corporations, labor unions, and extremely wealthy individuals — the three groups with the kind of financial firepower to singlehandedly catapult a candidate into office — can form groups that spend money with impunity.

The *Citizens United* judgment changed the election landscape, as evidenced by the results of the 2010 midterm elections, which saw Republicans — many of them members of the Republican Party's new Tea Party wing — retake the majority of the House of Representatives. Democrats also saw their majority decrease dramatically in the Senate.

Don't assume that *Citizens United* is a strictly partisan affair, however: Labor unions, traditionally supportive of Democratic candidates, were aggressive in forming PACs in preparation for the 2012 presidential election. In fact, *Citizens United* has been publicly opposed by — and supported by — both Democrats and Republicans.

Becoming beholden to financial supporters

Prior to *Citizens United,* campaign finance reform had built steadily and aggressively from 1971 to 2002. In 1971, the Federal Election Campaign Act required the disclosure of donors' identities and the amounts they contributed. In 2002 came the Bipartisan Campaign Reform Act, better known as the *McCain-Feingold Act* after the bill's primary sponsors, Republican John McCain and Democrat Russ Feingold.

For some people, the *Citizens United* case is an extremely regressive step in the path of campaign finance, as any and all groups can spend as much as they want without having to disclose their identities. For others, including prominent civil liberties groups, the case is an affirmation of free speech.

You may think that one positive effect of *Citizens United* is that it loosened the reins on campaign finance regulation so much that at least candidates can avoid illegal financial dealings. After all, if someone can support a political campaign without limit, and do so without being named, why not just use the PAC avenue to funnel money to the candidate of your choice?

Defying any logic, some candidates will still accept and spend money illegally, whether via embezzlement, unfair expenditure of public funds, or secret bribes taken in exchange for political influence. And if we're really being honest, the acceptance of nonpublic financial contributions from anybody quickly falls into an ethical gray area for a congressional candidate: "Do I do what's right in my heart and for the citizens of my district, or should I do what those who gave me money want?" If you want to stay in Congress for years, even decades, the answer to that question becomes even murkier.

What do you get for your money?

Money usually decides who wins an election. The more money you have in your coffers, the more people you can place on staff to devise strategy, manage a candidate's message, and conduct critical data polling about the trends of the electorate. Transportation and accommodations while campaigning are more easily and comfortably provided. More advertising can be placed on TV screens and front yards. More volunteers can be marshaled to help canvas district neighborhoods. Your general presence as a candidate increases dramatically.

Of course, the person with the most money isn't always the best person to represent a state or a congressional district. And the person who accepts the most financial contributions very likely arrives in the halls of Congress indebted to certain interests who helped him get there. But we're not writing a fairytale here; we're representing what actually happens. So until the next major reform to campaign finance occurs — until PACs are packed on ice, perhaps — this is the new reality of how someone becomes your senator or representative.

Chapter 6

The Presidency

. . . .

In This Chapter

▶ Figuring out a president's powers and limitations

▶ Raising money and running for office

▶ Getting a sense of the President's work routine

. . . .

*T*he leader of the free world. The commander-in-chief. The decider. The President of the United States has many titles, underscoring his central role in making and executing federal policy.

Although the Founding Fathers tried their utmost to ensure that the United States would not be led by a monarch like the one they rebelled against, the position of the presidency has unmistakably grown in power over the last two centuries of American history. Some historians have even deemed its modern incarnation the *Imperial Presidency*. But aside from increased influence and the occasional trappings of royalty, the President is still only one actor in the panoply of Washington policymakers.

In this chapter, we explain the President's duties and limitations, the role played by his staff, the ways that campaigning and fundraising affect a presidency, and what the chief executive of the United States does on a daily basis.

The Workings of the White House

The White House isn't merely a residence or presidential office; it's a formidable bureaucracy in its own right. As we explain in Chapter 2, the Executive Office of the President

(EOP) is the apex of the executive branch, where policy is crafted, advice is given, decisions are made, and the bureaucracy is managed. The EOP exists to support one man, who ultimately bears sole responsibility for the actions of his administration. President Harry S. Truman didn't shy away from this burden: His now-famous desk sign read simply, "The buck stops here."

Fulfilling the duties of office

Presidential pageantry, stage-managed press conferences, heavily scripted town hall events, smiling photos with sports teams . . . the images beamed across America sometimes suggest that the President is more cheerleader-in-chief than commander-in-chief. While the age of television tends to overemphasize these self-imposed presidential duties, he does actually have specific responsibilities laid out by the U.S. Constitution, which we introduce first.

Constitutional duties

Here are the constitutional duties of the presidency:

- ✔ **Serving as commander-in-chief:** Under the Constitution, the President is the commander-in-chief of the Army and Navy of the United States, as well as of "the Militia of the several States, when called into the actual service of the United States" — in other words, the National Guard. (The drafters of the Constitution, as forward-thinking as they were, didn't anticipate the Air Force.)

  The President does not have the power to declare war (that was left for Congress), but considering that the last formal declaration of war was in 1942, modern presidents certainly haven't shied away from exercising their powers as commander-in-chief.

- ✔ **Carrying out legislation:** As the head of the executive branch of the federal government, the President is responsible for ensuring that all the nation's laws are "faithfully executed." In other words, the President carries out the legislation enacted by Congress but cannot initiate legislation himself. (If he wants a piece of legislation introduced to Congress, he must find a sympathetic member of the House or Senate to do so.)

While constitutionally speaking the President is empow-
ered only to sign or veto legislation that Congress sends
to his desk, presidents have in recent years become
more assertive in interpreting legislation through the
use of *signing statements.* These statements often object
to the provisions of a particular law on constitutional
grounds and instruct executive branch officials how to
implement the legislation according to the President's
interpretation.

✔ **Setting foreign policy:** The President sets the foreign
policy of the United States and in that regard has the
authority, "by and with the consent of the Senate" (as
indicated by the concurrence of two-thirds of the senators present), to make treaties.

✔ **Appointing key personnel:** Subject to Senate confirmation, the President appoints ambassadors, justices
of the Supreme Court, and "all other Officers of the
United States."

✔ **Presenting the State of the Union:** The Constitution
instructs the President "from time to time to give to
the Congress information on the State of the Union and
recommend to their Consideration such Measures as he
shall judge necessary and expedient." The Constitution
does not require the President to deliver these reports
in person. In fact, the vast majority of State of the Union
reports have been delivered in written form.

More recently, of course, the State of the Union speech
has become a primetime television event, complete
with televised opposition party response and selected
special guests in the gallery featured by the President.
These days, the State of the Union address is given in late
January and is scheduled carefully to avoid conflicts with
the Super Bowl and the Academy Awards. (After all, the
size of the television audience is what matters!)

✔ **Pardoning felons:** Per the Constitution, the President
also can choose to pardon felons, or even to preemptively
pardon people who have not been convicted of any crime.
President Gerald Ford took this latter step when pardoning President Richard Nixon for any crimes that he may
have committed. Perhaps the most sweeping pardon of all
was President Andrew Johnson's pardon of soldiers who
fought for the Confederacy during the Civil War.

Self-imposed duties

The President also has many other self-imposed duties — some of the most enjoyable being throwing out the first baseball on opening day of the major league season, hosting hundreds of kids at the White House Easter Egg Roll, and pardoning the White House Thanksgiving turkey. He's also on hand for more solemn occasions, be it a funeral for a prominent American public figure or the aftermath of a major natural disaster.

In fact, much of what the President does today is self-imposed. Nothing in the Constitution says he must light the White House Christmas tree or even get involved in the nitty-gritty details of legislating. But the reality of today's presidency is that it's an all-encompassing role, and the personalities driven to run for President do not shy away from imposing themselves in all arenas once in office.

Knowing his limitations: Can one man change Washington?

Many presidents have come to Washington promising to shake up the city and fundamentally change the way it does business. They're not part of the much-maligned Washington establishment and don't mind ruffling a few feathers if necessary. But while presidents can make their mark on the city, they have all found themselves inevitably sucked into the usual maelstrom of Washington politicking.

Why the consistent and repeated failure to change business as usual in Washington? Because presidents compete with a slew of other actors who also play critical roles in policymaking. And while the President will occupy the White House for a maximum of eight years, the Washington establishment and veterans in Congress enjoy home turf advantage. Making a fundamental change of course in Washington is even more difficult than changing the course of a giant ocean liner. It happens only slowly and requires that the crew and captain work together.

As we explore in greater depth in Chapter 7, policymaking is an inclusive process, and its participants tend to jealously guard their own participation and prerogatives within the process. Presidents who step on too many toes often see their efforts stymied by these checks and balances. Woe betide the

President who gets on the wrong side of a grumpy senator, for example, because so-called *holds* allow a single senator to prevent any motion from being voted upon, whether it be a presidential nomination or critical piece of legislation. Presidents eventually realize that in order to actually get things done, they cannot avoid dealing with Washington on its own terms.

The sense of impotence and even besiegement in the face of other Washington power centers is by no means limited to the idealistic young presidents frustrated by their inability to enact their campaign promises. President Nixon once declared to Henry Kissinger, "Never forget. The press is the enemy. The establishment is the enemy. The professors are the enemy. . . . Write that on a blackboard 100 times and never forget it." And history hardly paints President Nixon as a naive idealist.

Even when presidents do take well-intentioned steps to try to change how Washington works for the better, critics are often quick to underline the unintended, even damaging consequences. Consider President Barack Obama's decision to restrict federally registered lobbyists from administration appointments and federal advisory committees (a policy that has had several prominent exemptions). It was lambasted by the Center for Lobbying in the Public Interest (CLPI) for having "done little to curb special interest influence in Washington" and "unintentionally harming public-interest advocacy and undermining the Administration's efforts to promote transparency and good government." According to a CLPI survey, nonprofit leaders described the restrictions as everything from "misguided" to "insidious," and 80 percent agreed that they were "harmful to the public interest."

Using the bully pulpit

Presidents have often tried to find ways to circumvent their policymaking competitors in Washington, and no method is more conspicuous (and audible) than the presidential bully pulpit. In fact, while the term *bully pulpit* is used today to describe any position that gives the occupant the ability to proclaim his views, it was invented by none other than President Theodore Roosevelt, who in speaking of the presidency once declared, "I suppose my critics will call that preaching, but I have got such a bully pulpit!"

Presidents use their bully pulpit to achieve many different objectives. Oftentimes, congressional gridlock convinces the President to call a prime time address to reach over Congress's head and speak directly with the American people, urging them to support his plans or at least taking the time to blame Congress for obstructionism. But he can really use the bully pulpit for any policy objective, whether it's supporting a particular piece of legislation, promoting investment in new technology, encouraging Americans to carpool and turn down their thermostats (President Jimmy Carter's gift to presidential rhetoric), or improving America's image in the world.

While presidents like to believe that their very words can sway the minds of millions, some research has called the effectiveness of the presidential bully pulpit into question. One academic who has been at the forefront of this line of inquiry, George C. Edwards III from Texas A&M University's Center for Presidential Studies, found little convincing evidence that presidential rhetoric had much effect on poll numbers.

Relying on his support team

In addition to his Cabinet and the thousands of political appointments throughout the federal government (see Chapter 2), the President relies heavily on the White House staff: his inside team of personal aides, who do not require Senate confirmation. The number of such aides is not specified by law but is limited by the size of the White House and a political sensitivity to the size of the White House budget.

The principal manager of the White House staff is the President's *Chief of Staff.* This person oversees the various operations within the White House, including congressional relations, public communications, access to the President, vetting of candidates for political appointments, policy advice, and political strategies. The position is enormously powerful, and presidents routinely assert that the Chief of Staff is subject to *executive privilege* (meaning not subject to congressional oversight).

In any hierarchical organization, the person who controls the paper flow to the executive also is very powerful. In the White House, the paper flow is managed by the Staff Secretary. The title sounds rather innocuous, but don't be fooled; this year's Staff Secretary can become next year's Chief of Staff.

The most influential advisors to the President may be difficult to determine by solely examining the EOP flowchart. Personalities and personal ties matter; old friends and colleagues who have stuck by the President through thick and thin may hold more sway than party stalwarts who have served under numerous administrations. Official titles also have a habit of becoming vaguer; Presidents George W. Bush and Barack Obama chose to designate their most trusted political confidants as merely *senior advisors.* Some presidential right-hand men, from John F. Kennedy's Ted Sorensen to George W. Bush's Karl Rove, have become famous public figures in their own right.

In an environment where hierarchies may matter little, having the President's ear is key, and bureaucratic infighting is fierce, it's not surprising that a less-than-cohesive team may emerge. President Abraham Lincoln's deft management of the "team of rivals" he assembled into a Cabinet during the Civil War is perhaps more the exception than the rule. Whenever you hear that an administration official is resigning to spend more time with his family, you can bet that some strategic leaks to the press will soon paint the official as someone who didn't quite bond with the President or wasn't a team player. Office politics can be nasty anywhere, and the EOP certainly isn't immune to them.

Indeed, closeness to the flame of power often results in getting scalded. Some White House chiefs of staff have learned the hard way. President Dwight D. Eisenhower's Chief of Staff, Sherman Adams, was forced to resign after it was revealed that he had accepted a vicuna coat from a businessman who was being investigated by the federal government. President Nixon's Chief of Staff, H.R. Haldeman, was forced to resign and ultimately convicted of crimes associated with the Watergate scandal. But other chiefs of staff have used that position as a stepping stone to political office. President Ford's Chief of Staff, Dick Cheney, subsequently became the 46th Vice President. And President Obama's first Chief of Staff, Rahm Emanuel, became the mayor of Chicago.

Governing from the bubble

Brian Williams: *This says you're in a bubble. You have a very small circle of advisors now. Is that true? Do you feel in a bubble?*

President George W. Bush: *No, I don't feel in a bubble.*

All rulers risk losing touch with the people they rule, and today's President, protected by a phalanx of Secret Service agents and handpicked supporters at every public event, inevitably finds himself in the so-called White House bubble. The bubble limits what the President knows and thus influences how he decides and acts. While each President finds himself in a bubble of one size or thickness, it tends to become a political liability only when it becomes apparent to voters that the President truly is isolated, even ignorant of what's really going on. Most Americans assume that the President has access to the best information available and that his advisors make sure he gets it, but that ain't necessarily so.

Touring the White House

The President's official residence and office is in the White House at 1600 Pennsylvania Avenue. Every President since John Adams has lived in the White House, which officially received that name from President Theodore Roosevelt. The White House was designed by Irish architect James Hoban. Completed in 1800, it was burned by British troops (along with the Capitol, the Treasury, and the Library of Congress) on August 24, 1814, in retaliation for American destruction of the Parliament Building and other property in York, then the provincial capital of Upper Canada. The outer shell of the White House survived the fire, and the building was restored in time for the inauguration of President James Monroe in 1817.

The White House contains both the private residence of the President and his family and the offices of the President and his staff, the latter inhabiting the West Wing, which is a rabbit warren of small offices but holds enormous prestige for its inhabitants. The West Wing also houses the Situation Room, where the President and his advisors meet during moments of national crises, especially foreign policy and military situations. The East Wing traditionally is the office area for the First Lady of the United States. And, of course, there is the Oval Office, the geometrically eponymous official office of the President, which dates from the presidency of William Howard Taft. Just outside the Oval Office is the Rose Garden, where numerous presidents have welcomed foreign dignitaries and American celebrities and have held press conferences. The Rose Garden was the site of the signing of the 1994 Israel-Jordan Treaty of Peace.

Some presidents, despite the inherent isolation of the job, try to break free from their small circles of advisors. President Kennedy, for example, was famous for reportedly calling midlevel desk officers in the State Department to get direct answers from bureaucrats who actually knew their subject matter. President Obama reportedly surfs the Internet to augment the information he receives through traditional channels.

Campaigning and Policymaking

> *Anybody who wants the Presidency so much that he'll spend two years organizing and campaigning for it is not to be trusted with the office.*
>
> — *Washington Post* journalist and commentator David Broder

Running for President is very expensive — and becoming increasingly so. In addition, it's time-consuming, involving many months (even years) of building name recognition, establishing policy stances, and trying to influence how people vote — particularly in so-called *swing states* that don't decisively favor either Republicans or Democrats. The process can be further complicated by the relationship of a candidate to the political party machine that must endorse him or her.

In this section, we briefly consider the influence of campaign donations on an administration's policies, the power wielded by voters in swing states, and the relationship between a presidential candidate and his or her political party.

Donating money and influencing policy

The Center for Responsive Politics estimated that the 2008 presidential campaigns cost $2.4 billion. The Obama campaign set a record for fundraising at $745 million.

The Federal Election Campaign Act (FECA), passed in 1971 and amended in 1974 and 2002, was aimed at curbing the influence of money in presidential elections by providing public funding for campaigns in return for candidates forgoing the collection of private contributions and accepting a limit on their campaign spending. The amount of the federal grant is adjusted for inflation. In 2008, each of the major candidates was eligible for $84.1 million. Senator John McCain accepted the federal money and its limitations, but Senator Obama declined.

Clearly, donors are critical to a candidate's success. President George W. Bush famously told a group of wealthy donors, "Some people call you the elite. I call you my base."

While quid pro quos are illegal, to say that donors have no effect on policy is simply untrue. There is a long and well-established tradition of appointing prominent presidential campaign donors as U.S. ambassadors, who (while not always the most influential officials) hold important posts that give them influence over federal policy. Donors may be appointed to other administration positions as well, or placed on presidential advisory committees.

Money also buys access. President Bill Clinton was criticized for allowing donors to sleep overnight in the Lincoln Bedroom, but he was hardly the first or last president to grant prominent supporters and fundraisers privileged access to the halls of power.

Concentrating disproportionate power in swing states

Most presidential aspirants strive to be elected, and most incumbents strive to be reelected. Inevitably, the electoral system exercises a strong influence over a presidential candidate's or incumbent's policy proposals. Under the current Electoral College, whereby presidents are elected indirectly by electors from each state, most states determine electors on a winner-takes-all basis. What this means in practice is that many states, which are either heavily Republican or heavily Democratic, are uncompetitive in a presidential election. Whichever party is assured the popular vote win in that state will take home all its electoral votes.

The corollary to this system is that a small number of competitive states (so-called *swing states*) exercise a disproportionate influence in choosing the presidential victor. And winning over the voters in these crucial swing states is the main objective of each presidential candidate.

Presidential policymaking, and thus federal policymaking, is influenced by swing state constituents. U.S. policy toward Cuba, for example, has been shaped in no small part by the anti-Castro views of the large Cuban American community in the swing state of Florida. U.S. trade policy has been influenced by generally free trade–skeptical union votes in rustbelt swing states like Ohio.

Nothing is inherently wrong or insidious about interest groups affecting U.S. policy. As we show in Chapter 3, policymaking is a vibrant and inclusive process. The Electoral College system simply encourages the presidential candidates to pay additional attention to certain interest groups whose strategic location gives them greater electoral significance than they would otherwise enjoy.

Dealing with party politics

Parliamentary systems of government often lead to hierarchical parties. For the party in power, the head of the party is the prime minister, and decisions flow down from him. If party members no longer support him, they vote him out and choose someone else.

U.S. political parties are less hierarchical and usually have multiple centers of power. While the President (or presidential candidate) is considered to be the head of his party, he still must win over, or at least deal with, other powerful individuals and groups to first win his party's nomination. Only then can he hope to win the presidency and implement his legislative agenda successfully.

Besides party leaders in Congress, presidents and presidential candidates must strive to satisfy powerful interest groups and voting blocs that make up their party's base of support. The balancing act between cooperating with one's party in Congress, satisfying various political constituencies, standing fast to one's principles, and achieving one's objectives in office sometimes proves impossible to sustain. President Lyndon B. Johnson acknowledged that his party could lose an important constituency by his signing of the Civil Rights Act of 1964, supposedly remarking, "We have lost the South for a generation." Ultimately, presidents must determine when to accommodate their party, when to make compromises, and when to go it alone.

A Day in the Life

What does the President do in a typical day — if such a thing exists? These days, you can actually check the President's official schedule on the White House website: www.whitehouse. gov. (Ain't technology grand?)

The President's official day begins with the President's Daily Brief, which is a highly classified document prepared by the Director of National Intelligence. It provides the President with sensitive intelligence on international matters and events. The material is available to other very senior officials on a strictly need-to-know basis.

The President then moves into a series of meetings or events. Often, this part of his day includes a briefing by one of his Cabinet officers or White House staff. He may also have meetings with White House staff and congressional leaders concerning the President's legislative strategy.

Most days also involve delivering remarks to one or more groups of citizens — everything from a roundtable of educators on raising high school performance, to business people on American competitiveness, to a thank-you to volunteers who responded to a natural disaster.

Various press events also are part of the schedule — not just formal, prime time presidential press conferences, but also press *scrums* at which he can deliver a quick message to the public on an individual issue or respond quickly to some press story. Other press events may include congratulating the winning World Series or Super Bowl team.

Other important events include meetings with foreign leaders, which may include hosting a state dinner (or taking the Russian president to a local hamburger joint, which President Obama did in 2010).

The President's out-of-town schedule is usually grueling. It runs the gamut from official visits to important allied countries, to participation in international meetings such as the United Nations General Assembly each fall, to political events in key states.

The vice presidency

The Vice Presidency is sort of like the last cookie on the plate. Everybody insists he won't take it, but somebody always does.

— Bill Vaughn

Taking that last cookie makes sense. Fourteen men who took the vice presidential cookie subsequently became president: nine due to the death or resignation of the President, and five by direct election. (Of the veeps who succeeded to the highest office, only Thomas Jefferson served two full terms as president.)

The vice presidency is not always the most stimulating or rewarding political position. Constitutionally, vice presidents preside over the U.S. Senate and cast the deciding vote in case of a tie, and they also represent the President at state funerals around the world. Other than that, they don't have many mandated duties, which is why John Adams, our first Vice President, called it "the most insignificant office that ever the invention of man contrived." Daniel Webster turned down the office of Vice President, declaring, "I do not propose to be buried until I am actually dead."

However, especially in modern times, the Vice President can have substantial influence depending upon his relationship with the President. Both Al Gore and Dick Cheney had important, substantive roles in their administrations. (In contrast, Franklin D. Roosevelt's number two, Harry Truman, came into office not knowing about the Manhattan Project's atomic bomb.)

The Constitution stipulates that the powers and duties of the President devolve to the Vice President "in case of the removal of the President from office, or of his Death, Resignation, or Inability to discharge the Powers and Duties" of the Office. The Constitution does not set out eligibility requirements for the Vice President, but obviously a Vice President could not succeed to the presidency unless he or she met the eligibility requirements for that office.

His duties also include signing legislation and international agreements, issuing Executive Orders to carry out various governmental actions or measures to implement laws, and nominating officials for Senate confirmation.

While all presidents seek to control their schedules, the sheer enormity of the issues that tend to hit the Oval Office all at once turns him into a firefighter of sorts. Imagine a day in which the President must deal with an intelligence report of a planned terrorist attack, a crisis in the Middle East, dire financial news from Europe, a domestic hot-button issue like healthcare legislation, looming budget and national debt issues . . . Such crises all have to be dealt with pretty much at the same time, and each of them is very important and difficult. It's easy to understand why self-imposed (and perhaps therapeutic) presidential duties such as throwing out the first baseball on opening day work their way onto the schedule as well.

Chapter 7

Policymaking

● ●

In This Chapter

▶ Crafting a policy idea and introducing it to decision makers

▶ Using advocacy to help shape policy

▶ Creating federal laws and regulations

▶ Checking and balancing how policies are enacted

▶ Realizing the policy power of Washington's establishment

● ●

*P*olicymaking is Washington's raison d'être. It's what happens when the federal government, elected officials, industry representatives, interest groups, think tanks, the media, foreign governments, international institutions, and a host of other actors collide to brainstorm, develop, and implement federal policy on nearly every issue imaginable. Some people liken it to making sausage, which is the quintessential messy process. We'd argue that policymaking is far more complicated than making a sausage — and probably a lot messier.

In preceding chapters, we discuss the principal players in Washington's policymaking game and the unique roles that they each play. This chapter combines a bit of information about each to illustrate the policymaking process as a whole.

Realizing That Anyone Can Think Up New Policy

Policy is not made in a vacuum. It isn't generated fully formed in the secret laboratories of policy wonks plugging away in Washington think tanks — at least not always. Nor is it restricted to the traditional legislative branch. Rather, policy ideas can originate in many different places and take on many different forms. Domestic policy can originate with either the President or the Congress, but often its true genesis can be traced outside of government. Foreign policy can be proactive — seeking to launch new international initiatives or build new foreign relationships — or reactive — responding to the actions or requests of a foreign government or leader or simply reacting to a change in circumstances (such as the death of a longtime leader or the overthrow of a government in power).

Truly anybody can think up a new federal policy. But not all policy is good policy, and not every policy idea leads to action. In fact, most policy ideas never leave the confines of the minds that dream them up. (Perhaps we should be thankful for that; not all dreams need be realized.)

If policy ideas are just as likely to originate from a top-flight think tank as they are from a veteran legislator or imaginative lobbyist, why do some ideas become policy while others don't? Simply put, because ideas are not enough. Ideas are a dime a dozen, no matter what a highly paid and highly vague strategist-for-hire may tell you. Navigating the policymaking cycle successfully is what distinguishes the daydreams from the future policies of the federal government.

Getting Ideas to the Policymakers

This section explains the first steps in the policymaking process, which are identifying the key stakeholders, making them aware of the policy idea, and helping them understand what various interested parties think about the proposed policy.

Recognizing the policy triangle

Making policy is a complicated process that's often riddled by compromises, half-baked ideas, and haphazardness. While the sausage-making analogy is often used, a slightly more elegant model to help visualize the key stakeholders involved in the policymaking process is the *policy triangle*. Three key stakeholders join together to form the triangle's sides:

- ✔ The White House
- ✔ Congress
- ✔ The private sector/interest groups

Each group represents the interests of a specific constituency, and sometimes the constituencies overlap. In the policy arena, the three major groups are constantly interacting to fine-tune policy objectives and tactics.

 Keep in mind that the first two sides of the triangle have the ability to place policy items on the government's agenda. Though the third side does not directly produce policy, it engages consistently with the first two sides in the policymaking process.

None of the three groups is monolithic. Congress, for example, splinters into Democrats, Republicans, Independents, and shifting coalitions within these demarcations. Within the three major groups, subgroups sometimes form alliances and coalitions to promote common views. Other times, interests differ so strongly (perhaps for partisan reasons or because of differences over substance) that some subgroups seek to block the actions of others. The constellation of players changes according to the issue being debated.

Putting the idea on the decision-makers' agenda

Within the policy triangle, members of the White House staff and Congress have a distinct advantage: As presidential appointees or elected representatives, they are policymakers. By no means does this mean that they can make policy on a whim; even policymakers must successfully navigate the laborious policymaking process. But they're in a position to initiate policy ideas from within the federal government.

The private sector and interest groups, while undoubtedly critical participants in the policymaking process, approach government policymaking from the outside. To push a policy agenda, they must persuade someone in the White House or Congress to take the idea and run with it. To accomplish this persuasion, they use a method called *advocacy,* which we explain next.

Employing Advocacy to Influence Policy Decisions

If you've read the earlier chapters, you're well aware that the private sector and interest groups, the third side of the policymaking triangle, play a huge role in Washington. As we explain in Chapters 3 and 4, lobbyists, think tanks, activists, diplomats, international organizations, and the media all have an influence. A lone citizen picking up the telephone can impact policy, as can the largest corporations and their legions of professional lobbyists and lawyers.

Together, the diverse players interested in influencing policy all participate in the policymaking process through advocacy, which is a critical element in the government decision-making process. Advocacy is employed to influence any and all decisions by policymakers, as diverse as spending money on new infrastructure, banning certain food additives, and pressing a foreign government on a particular issue of concern.

Later in the chapter, we examine two major policymaking processes — passing laws and writing regulations — and see how advocacy is used to influence their outcomes. Here, we focus on defining what advocacy is and exploring how it's most effectively employed.

Defining our terms: Advocacy and lobbying

Advocacy means taking steps to influence policy. It can be broad-based and focused on changing public opinion on a given issue, or it can be extremely specific and focused on changing the opinion of a single legislator or regulator. Most advocacy falls somewhere between these two extremes.

In the United States, advocacy from interested parties has become part and parcel of how the government makes informed decisions. In fact, our government views input from outside sources and stakeholders as essential and has established formal rulemaking processes for obtaining stakeholder views in a systematic manner. Integrating the viewpoints and expertise of all stakeholders on a given issue helps to ensure that the outcome — whether legislation, administrative rules and regulations, or policy — is well balanced.

Is there any difference between advocacy and lobbying? The answer, like much of what occurs in Washington, is complicated. Advocacy is generally considered to encompass a broader array of policy activities than lobbying. Numerous interests actively advocate, including individuals, non-governmental organizations (NGOs), business groups, academic and research institutions, key opinion leaders, foreign governments, and international organizations. Advocacy can be conducted by a third party expressing support for, or opposition to, an issue or by a direct representative of a particular interest or cause.

Legally, lobbying seems to have a more specific definition, but that doesn't mean the definition isn't still the subject of debate. The Lobbying Disclosure Act, which we explain in Chapter 3, contains specific rules that describe when an individual is required to register publicly as a lobbyist. The Internal Revenue Service defines lobbying as activities that influence legislation — not activities that influence decisions by executive officials or general advocacy activities in the public policy arena. (The IRS gets involved in the definition business because it limits the amount of lobbying done by nonprofits that wish to qualify for tax-exempt status.)

While some Washingtonians could write you a dissertation on how advocacy differs from lobbying, others use the terms interchangeably. The ultimate aim of both activities is the same: to influence policy. Therefore, we don't get hung up on the semantic differences here. Just keep in mind that some people can't say the word *lobbying* without spitting in contempt, so to be safe, you can use the word *advocacy* as a catchall euphemism.

Distinguishing indirect and direct advocacy

Two main types of advocacy are employed:

- ✔ **Grass-roots/indirect advocacy:** This type of advocacy seeks to motivate the general public to communicate a position to government officials. Grass-roots advocacy can be done through protests, the media (mainstream, social, or both), and letter/e-mail campaigns from the public. It also includes indirect ways of swaying the policy debate. Think tanks, for instance, often issue policy reports and recommendations that are (occasionally) read by policy-making stakeholders and thereby shape the debate.

- ✔ **Direct advocacy:** This type of advocacy is normally accomplished through these means:

    - One-on-one meetings and contacts with members of the administration or Congress.

    - Formal government processes (where they exist).

    - Letters sent directly from private sector or special interest organizations to policymakers.

    - Billboards in D.C. metro stations aimed at attracting the attention of congressional staffers and administration officials. (For example, the Pentagon metro station is essentially one big advertisement for the defense industry.)

    - Hill briefings to converse with (and educate) members of Congress and their staffs.

    - Hearings in congressional committees where public witnesses can testify on an issue.

    Companies often conduct direct advocacy through like-minded third-party groups (such as trade or business associations, patient groups, or key opinion leaders). Sometimes one company takes the lead; other times, an association or Chamber of Commerce represents a group of companies on behalf of the industry. Other stakeholder groups (such as environmental, human rights, and animal rights groups) employ the same methods to advocate for their positions.

Building an advocacy message

There are several keys to building an effective advocacy message:

- ✔ **The advocate should be able to speak authoritatively about all aspects of the organization he represents.** Advocates are expected to be knowledgeable about how their organization has an impact on the specific issue in question. Integrating these facts into letters, requests for meetings, and meeting talking points helps to build the rationale for why the organization is an important stakeholder on the issue and why its voice should be heard.

- ✔ **The advocate should be well versed on the overall issue.** This person must know not only the perspective he is representing but also the counterarguments and similar perspectives of other stakeholders advocating on the same issue.

- ✔ **The advocate should research the policymakers he hopes to approach.** This step may involve assessing the policymakers' overall understanding of the issue, as well as their interests and constraints.

- ✔ **The advocate should customize the message to the particular policymakers being contacted.** Based on his research, he should tailor his pitch by keeping the policymakers' specific interests and constraints in mind.

Practicing a powerful delivery

Determining how to deliver the advocacy message is just as critical as crafting the message itself. Deciding who will convey the message is very important. Sometimes stakeholders with similar concerns and perspectives may choose to join voices in a coalition to approach a government entity. Often, the collective voice is more powerful than a single entity in attracting visibility to an issue. In other instances, an individual organization may choose to approach the government entity on its own in order to differentiate its voice from the pack.

Smart advocates are also careful in selecting which officials they approach. In most cases, more than one agency, office, or official is responsible for the same issue. Obtaining a strong understanding of which entities have the influence to affect the outcome of a specific issue ensures that time and resources are not wasted chasing rabbit trails that lead nowhere.

Policy benefits versus unintended consequences

Even well-intended and well-analyzed policies can bring about unintended consequences. An action meant to bring about one set of reactions can inadvertently create incentives that lead to another set of unforeseen costs and adverse effects.

For example, when the U.S. auto industry began to experience competition from cheaper, more fuel-efficient Japanese cars, the industry lobbied U.S. policymakers to help it remain competitive. Its efforts brought about the 1981 voluntary export restraint (VER) agreement with Japan, which limited Japanese auto exports to 1.68 million cars annually. Though the agreement did bring fewer Japanese cars into the United States, it also incentivized the Japanese to export bigger and more expensive cars. This paved the way for Japanese luxury brands such as Lexus, Acura, and Infiniti, which soon outcompeted American luxury brands. In addition, the Japanese auto industry began establishing factories in the United States that produced Japanese-brand cars, defeating the purpose of the VER.

A more recent example is that of U.S. government subsidies for biofuel production. Though they're intended to reduce greenhouse gas emissions, critics of the subsidies say that ethanol, made mainly from corn, has diverted grain (and associated land use) from food to fuel. Subsidized ethanol subsequently helps drive up the price of grain, which may be good for farmers and rural communities but bad for city dwellers who must pay more for the food they eat.

These examples show that even the most careful and deliberate policymaker may not be able to anticipate the full effects of a policy's implementation. This makes the case even greater for public participation, open debate, and full transparency in the policymaking process. The more information and greater the variety of stakeholder input policymakers have, the more likely they are to think of all the possible variables and outcomes that could result from a policy. A system that allows interest groups with different perspectives to voice concerns throughout each step of a law's implementation can help avoid the most harmful unintentional consequences when implementing a policy.

Finally, smart advocates also carefully gauge timing and sequencing, knowing that when and in what order to approach a decision maker is just as important as what is said. Sometimes taking the lead on an emerging issue necessitates early engagement with multiple players. Other times, waiting for further clarification from the government or until a broad-based coalition can be built is more effective.

Getting a reality check from Washington insiders

Civil servants at the bureaucratic level are often the real issue experts in Washington, having devoted much of their careers to studying and following a particular policy area. They have the institutional memory on policies, knowing all the twists and turns that have occurred in formulating a particular policy across past administrations. As a result, they can advise advocates regarding what arguments will or won't work best in the current policy environment in Washington. Therefore, cultivating good relationships with knowledgeable civil servants can save advocates considerable time, money, and effort in pushing for particular approaches.

In Washington, the same (or similar) ideas often come around time and time again, and many civil servants have been through one or more iterations. If you plan to be an advocate, civil servants can help you by pointing out the mistakes of the past so that you avoid committing them again, as well as teaching you what to do right this time so that your policy effort succeeds in the current environment.

Turning Bills into Laws

Civics textbooks, at least for the younger crowd, often concentrate on the step-by-step process whereby a bill becomes a law. This is undoubtedly an integral process in Washington policymaking. But instead of conceiving of it as an assembly line constantly churning out new laws of the land, politicians, lobbyists, and other participants understand that the policymaking process is fluid, with many sidetracks, dead ends, and feedback loops. Interventions at key moments by specific players can spell the success or failure of an initiative. That's what advocacy is all about: planning and implementing effective interventions. Political gamesmanship and bargaining may hold up one bill for the sake of another, even if little or no linkage exists between the two.

In broad terms, a bill follows a similar path through both the House of Representatives and the Senate:

1. **The bill is drafted.** The drafting process is an important time for stakeholders of all stripes to ensure that their input is included in the bill's text. The ideas behind a bill can originate from any part of the policy triangle, but the bill must be proposed to a member of Congress, who is uniquely able to introduce legislation.

2. **A member of Congress introduces the bill, and the clerk assigns it a number.** This is a key moment in the bill's lifetime. Most bills never receive press attention after the introduction, if they ever did in the first place. Members of Congress often issue press releases regarding a bill's introduction, both to generate publicity for it and to create a paper trail for their reelection campaigns. Other stakeholders who support or oppose the bill may get their opinions out too, either to make sure the bill is dead on arrival or to mobilize support to see it through to the next round.

3. **The bill is referred to committee and (possibly) subcommittee.** The Speaker of the House and the presiding officer in the Senate are responsible for assigning a bill to a committee in their respective chambers. The committee chair may then assign it to a subcommittee.

   Committee assignments are sometimes obvious; for example, the ratification of a free trade agreement falls under the House Ways and Means or Senate Finance subcommittees for trade. But often, which committee has jurisdiction over a bill is less clear-cut. Because committees can bring newly proposed legislation to a screeching halt, supporters naturally favor assigning a bill to a committee in which it's likely to receive the most support.

4. **Committee hearings are held.** A committee hearing is the primary method for members of Congress to

learn about an issue. Hearings usually include a panel of stakeholders from different sectors who discuss the many aspects of the bill in consideration. Hearings are usually required to be publicly accessible unless specific sensitivities, such as national security concerns, come into play.

Most bills never leave this stage. Instead they are *tabled,* which means set aside and likely never looked at again. Therefore, supporters and opponents of the bill, whether they're in the government (such as administration officials) or outside (such as interest groups), may lobby fiercely at this stage. Likewise, some members of Congress will lobby their colleagues at this stage and may demonstrate their support by signing up as cosponsors of the bill.

5. **The subcommittee and full committee members mark up the bill.** When hearings are complete, subcommittee and committee members examine the bill line by line and offer amendments. Stakeholders who were not entirely satisfied with the original version may leverage this process to recommend adding new provisions, deleting existing ones, or even embarking on a full rewrite. Politics are naturally at play: While some amendments may be intended to genuinely improve the bill (at least in the proposing member's opinion), less politically palatable amendments known as *poison pills* may be offered with the intent to wreck the whole process and force supporters to vote against their own legislation later on.

6. **The bill is reported out and calendared.** The bill and a written report about it prepared by the committee are sent to the relevant chamber and placed on its calendar. In the House, the Rules Committee plays a pivotal role in deciding how a bill will be considered, such as how amendments may be added and how much time will be allowed for debate.

7. **The bill is read on the floor of the chamber, and amendments are debated.** As with the committee process, floor procedures are used by supporters in Congress to try to push a bill to a vote with minimum commotion and by opponents to effectively kill it in its tracks. This step is the final chance for stakeholders to influence the text of a bill before it goes to a vote.

8. **The bill goes to a full vote.** Like any vote, be it for student council or U.S. president, congressional votes are moments when each side scrambles to mobilize supporters and make sure they show up to make their opinions count. While private sector and special interest groups obviously cannot vote themselves, they work to galvanize support within Congress, the media, and public opinion. Lobbyists also get the chance to see whether their hard work actually changed any minds.

9. **A bill that passes goes to conference committee.** The House and Senate must both pass the same bill for it to be forwarded to the President's desk. But at this stage, they likely have passed similar but still different pieces of legislation. To reconcile the differences, an ad hoc committee of members from both chambers (a *conference*) comes together and negotiates a common text.

   Once again, this stage is an opportunity for all legs of the policy triangle to weigh in with the House members and senators involved in the process to influence the outcome. Entirely new provisions may be quietly inserted into a bill even if they were never considered by either the House or Senate.

10. **The House and Senate vote on the revised bill.** After the conference committee hammers out a common text, both chambers vote on the revised bill. If the bill is approved, it's then delivered to the President's desk.

11. **The President signs or vetoes the bill.** The White House is not spared from the lobbying onslaught that engulfs Congress. Nowadays, presidents rarely use their veto power and generally telegraph ahead of time how they will decide upon a particular bill. Even if he signs a bill into law, a president often uses so-called *signing statements* to attach his own interpretation to the measure, which can affect how it's implemented.

   If a president vetoes a bill, Congress may override the veto with a two-thirds majority in each chamber.

12. **The bill becomes law.** The policymaking process doesn't end when a new piece of legislation comes into force. Opponents often shift gears and begin campaigning for a law's amendment or repeal. Supporters stay focused to ensure that it is implemented as

expected. In fact, laws often leave it up to federal bureaucrats and regulators to determine the exact way in which it will be applied. Drafting such regulations is another key element of Washington's policymaking process, which we discuss next.

Writing Regulations to Support the Laws

Congress sets the framework of a broad policy mandate through legislation. Federal agencies then flesh out the policy supporting this mandate through the creation of more detailed regulations. For example, Congress may pass a new law that requires cosmetic companies to use safe and approved ingredients, but the Food and Drug Administration (FDA) is responsible for issuing regulations that let companies know exactly what this law means for their production going forward. The FDA may publish a list of approved ingredients that companies can use, for example, or require certain tests or approvals to satisfy the new law.

The *public comments* process in the United States allows the stakeholders on a given issue to provide input when the details of a particular policy are being formed. For many stakeholders, influencing how an agency writes a rule or regulation is much more important than influencing a bill under deliberation in Congress because often the devil is in the details.

The Code of Federal Regulations

The Code of Federal Regulations (CFR) is the public register of the permanent rules and regulations established by federal agencies. The Federal Register publishes proposed regulations, changes to existing rules, solicitations for comments, and final rules. The Federal Register not only allows citizens to participate in the policymaking process but also serves as an official journal to document the approved acts of the U.S. government. The website www.regulations.gov is the publicly searchable online database of U.S. government regulations from nearly 300 federal agencies.

Government agencies usually publish draft regulations or changes to existing regulations before calling for public comments. Stakeholders formally submit their comments, which are then made public and searchable online. In subsequent versions and revisions of the regulation in question, agencies (at their discretion) may incorporate stakeholder input into the final draft. Using the example of the hypothetical "safe cosmetics ingredients" bill, companies may submit comments on ways to tweak and amend the regulation so that it is most effective in providing consumer safety and least inhibitive of the companies' marketing or business operations.

Wielding Influence beyond Laws and Regulations

Understanding how laws and regulations are crafted with the input of a diversity of stakeholders is important. But in the broadest sense, federal policy is hardly limited to these written texts, and participants in the policymaking process often have different objectives besides influencing a particular bill or regulation. Convincing a House member or senator to write a letter to the President on your behalf, getting a prominent administration official to include a particular phrase in a speech, persuading a bureaucrat to concentrate on a hitherto overlooked issue — these are but a few examples of the kinds of objectives a stakeholder in the policymaking process may aim to achieve.

Spotting Checks and Balances in Policy Implementation

Checks and balances are a core tenet of the U.S. political system, written in by the Founding Fathers. The three branches of government check on each other and balance each other so that no single entity can amass a disproportionate amount of decision-making power.

In this section, we explain some crucial checks and balances that help ensure that policies are implemented in appropriate (and intended) ways.

Congressional oversight: Keeping the executive branch in check

One key function of Congress is to oversee executive branch operations; the many committees of Congress monitor and supervise the ways in which federal agencies implement policy. This oversight focuses on a couple key issues:

✔ Are federal agencies carrying out their mandates as directed by congressional legislation?

✔ Are these same agencies conducting their daily functions in line with congressional intent as outlined in the legislative history, floor debate, and other statements developed at the time a law was under consideration by the House and the Senate?

Some of the most famous (and scandalous) events in U.S. political history — the McCarthy Communism investigations, Watergate, and Iran-Contra — unfolded in congressional committee hearings.

Congress accomplishes the necessary checks and balances in various ways:

✔ To uncover fraud, waste, and abuse in government spending, Congress holds regular hearings in which agency heads respond directly to the questions and concerns of members of Congress under whose committee jurisdiction their respective agencies fall.

✔ The Government Performance and Results Act of 1993 requires that federal agencies consult with Congress on their performance on a regular basis. Agencies submit annual reports to Congress, outlining their performance plans and goals and summarizing results achieved (usually for the most recent and upcoming fiscal years).

✔ Some agencies have *inspectors general* who must report on a regular basis to the relevant congressional committees on agency performance or shortcomings.

✔ Congressional committees may, at their discretion, hold formal hearings to hear testimony from responsible agency officials (usually the politically appointed agency head) about topics or programs of particular interest.

✔ At times, congressional committee staff may meet informally with key agency personnel to discuss agency activities that are particularly important to senior committee members. If these informal contacts lead members of Congress to suspect that agency performance is lacking or deviating from congressional intent, they can lead to formal hearings or investigations.

✔ Individual legislators may express concerns directly to agency officials through letters, phone calls, or e-mails from staff, or through public statements.

✔ Congressional investigative bodies such as the U.S. Government Accountability Office (GAO) can issue detailed reports about federal agency performance and effectiveness. Agencies being investigated often meet with GAO staff to answer questions and may submit written comments in response to issued reports.

Clearly, members of Congress and the staff of federal agencies have a lot of interaction. To try to make the interaction as smooth as possible, and to coordinate its response to any concerns that are raised, each federal agency maintains a congressional affairs office.

The interagency process

Another example of checks and balances is the way in which the different parts of a single branch of government interact. In the executive branch, agencies that have overlapping jurisdiction over a policy issue must coordinate with one another through the *interagency process.*

An example of the interagency process is the multilayered decision-making process of U.S. foreign policy. In the role of central foreign policy coordinator is the National Security Council (NSC). The National Security Advisor (NSA) is the personal presidential advisor responsible for the NSC agenda, meeting preparations, records, and distribution of NSC decisions. In a larger capacity, the NSA is responsible for ensuring that the President has the resources to make a fully informed decision, providing him (and someday her) with not only the available policy options but also the risks, opportunities, and political and practical feasibility associated with each option.

At the most senior level, the interagency process is reflected by the *Principals Committee* (PC), which is chaired by the NSA. PC membership is up to the President; under the Obama administration, it has included the Secretaries of State, Treasury, Defense, Energy, and Homeland Security; the Attorney General; the Director of the Office of Management and Budget; the Ambassador to the United Nations; the President's Chief of Staff; the Director of National Intelligence; and the Chairman of the Joint Chiefs of Staff. Often, other key Cabinet-level officials are invited to attend PC meetings when their issue of responsibility is being discussed. For example, when international economic or trade policy is on the agenda, additional participants may include the Secretary of Commerce, U.S. Trade Representative, or Secretary of Agriculture.

However, the interagency process is much more complex than just holding meetings among the top Cabinet-level officials. Immediately below the PC is the Deputies Committee (DC), made up of the deputies or relevant undersecretaries of the executive agencies. The DC is responsible for managing the work of the interagency working groups at the staff level and making sure that the issues that are finally raised for PC and NSC review have been thoroughly evaluated.

Historically, the DC level is where most policy decisions are made before the PC's review and President's decision. Usually, the issues that are raised to the PC level are very controversial or have major national security implications.

Beneath the DC (adding more layers to our already-multilayered process) are interagency working groups or policy coordinating committees. These working groups are made up of issue experts, often with a regional or functional focus. Depending on the nature of the issues and responsibilities, these working groups meet regularly or only when an issue requires reconciliation or more than one agency's involvement in implementing decisions.

Making and implementing policy through the interagency process involves shifting factions and coalitions, just as you find in Congress (although party labels may not be at play in the interagency process). This reality creates built-in checks and balances within the executive branch — and, on occasion, gridlock. It also gives lobbyists the opportunity to insert themselves into the process by staying in touch with the agencies involved. Smart lobbyists find out where interagency players stand on a specific issue, identify who is driving that issue, and launch targeted advocacy to support or stall it.

Untangling the Policy Web: The Power of Washington Insiders

Nobody ever said that Washington was a simple place. The diversity of stakeholders involved in the policymaking process, and the innumerable forms of interaction among stakeholders within government and between government and the public, suggests something akin to a tangled web.

The people who understand this tangle are the ones who have been around it longest: the Washington establishment. They have burrowed deepest into the bowels of the federal bureaucracy, jumped around its assortment of law firms or think tanks, and probably spent a spell or two on the Hill. Few of them court publicity. Most spend their careers in relative obscurity, known only to the small circle of professionals in their particular area of focus.

Occasionally, the spotlight hits one of their number, perhaps appointed to a distinguished administration post or (in rare cases) disgraced for crossing the line. Sooner rather than later, the public attention dissipates, and the members of the establishment continue with their jobs as usual.

At times when the public identifies important flaws in the health of our democracy, be it increasing partisan polarization or the corrosive influence of money in politics, the members of the establishment, especially those who openly register as lobbyists, are easy targets. Some are criticized as influence peddlers, others as special interests.

The Washington establishment is not blameless, though neither is it uniquely culpable. Despite its many inefficiencies and occasionally subpar outcomes, the policymaking process in Washington is an inclusive process, which simultaneously accounts for its fairness and frustration. And without the individuals who have spent their lives learning what levers to pull and what gears to turn, the whole process would likely come to a grinding halt. They, and now you, know how Washington actually works.

Chapter 8

Ten Ways to Participate in Washington Policymaking

In This Chapter

▶ Aiming to become a Washington insider

▶ Wielding influence from the outside

*E*ver wonder what makes the people who wield influence in Washington different from you? Are they smarter? Taller? Better at telling jokes? Much of the time, the key factor that distinguishes Washington insiders from the rest of the world is drive. If you're driven to get involved, to share your ideas, and to try to wield some influence, chances are that you can make your voice heard in a policy debate. In this chapter, we suggest ten ways to turn your drive into action.

Be Informed

Before you even consider getting your hands dirty playing the policymaking game, it's important to become knowledgeable about the issues at hand. Your voice will be more respected if you have your facts straight and can marshal convincing evidence to support your arguments and recommendations.

You don't need to sit through elementary civics class again, but reading the Washington-related stories in one (or all) of the major national papers is a prerequisite. Tuning into a 24-hour cable news channel is also a quick way to become acquainted with the media story du jour, but don't rely on this medium for the nuances of federal policymaking. C-SPAN is where that action really happens. When you're up to speed on the basics, page (or click) through Washington-focused political papers, which tend to get deeper into the weeds of congressional procedure and the intricate debates playing out among Congress, the White House, and other stakeholders.

After taking these steps, you should have a better feeling for what issues you are most passionate about and know where you'd like to focus your attention. Find out what think tanks or niche media outlets are writing about your issue, and if you're in the Washington area, consider attending some of the innumerable seminars, conferences, and other gatherings. On a daily basis, Washington is buzzing with in-depth discussions on foreign policy, economics, healthcare, and the full range of other issues. More policy debate and clashing of ideas goes on outside of government than within it.

Run for Congress (Or Join a Staff)

Call it old-fashioned, but if you want to craft policy, consider positioning yourself to become a policymaker. Running for office isn't for the faint of heart (or light of wallet), but someone has to do it. While you'll develop expertise in specific fields of policy, likely correlated to the committees you sit on in Congress, as a legislator you can really dabble in whatever you want. As a freshman, you'll hardly be running the show; seniority rules ensure that you face a (decades) long slog to the top. But you can still interrogate administration officials and bureaucrats, vote your conscience (or party line), and enjoy the minor trappings of power. You're certain to get a front-row seat to how policymaking works; in fact, you're likely to be hounded by lobbyists of all stripes.

But maybe you don't have the money, charisma, or drive to run for office. That's okay, because an alternative to being an elected legislator is to finagle your way onto a legislator's staff. Congressional employees range from lowly interns to formidable chiefs of staff, and while members of the House and Senate fundraise, pontificate on television, and shake hands with constituents, staffers ensure that Congress actually does its homework. They brainstorm policy ideas, write legislation, negotiate behind closed doors, interact with stakeholders, and advise senators and congressmen on how to vote. Legislators rely heavily on their staffs, and after assuming such responsibility (often granted at a young age), many staffers use their Capitol Hill experience to launch successful Washington careers.

Join the Bureaucracy

Federal bureaucrats are vital cogs in the policymaking machine. They write regulations, enforce the rules, and interact with all manner of public and private sector stakeholders. If Congress is for generalists, the bureaucracy is for experts. If you work for the National Oceanic and Atmospheric Administration, you probably won't become an expert in terrorist networks in Southeast Asia, but you might just become the world's preeminent expert on seafood regulations.

The standard gateway into the federal bureaucracy is the website www.USAJOBS.gov, which lists open positions across the myriad departments and agencies. However, some special organizations, like the U.S. Foreign Service and the CIA, have their own unique hiring process that candidates must go through to be considered for employment. And if you're after one of the prized political appointments, you'd better start thumbing through your copy of the Plum Book (see Chapter 2) and get your administration contacts on the phone. Better yet, start working for a presidential campaign.

Contact Your Member of Congress

"I'm just an ordinary citizen," you might say. "I don't have time to run for political office, I'm too old to join the gaggle of 20-somethings in line for their first congressional staff job, and I certainly don't have the patience to become a lifelong bureaucrat."

Don't worry. You still have plenty of opportunities to participate in U.S. policymaking. Almost all citizens, no matter where
they live, are already represented in the policymaking debate
through their local House member and senators (sorry, D.C.
residents and Puerto Ricans). The most basic and fundamental way you normally influence the policymaking debate is
by voting. By pulling that lever or punching that chad (don't
leave it hanging!), you are taking a clear stand on what policy
direction you want the country to move in and whom you
want to represent you in Washington.

But voting isn't always enough. Regardless of what was
debated during a political campaign, Congress is always grap-
pling with a barrage of new issues and decisions. The easiest
way to let your senator or representative know what you want
her to do is to tell her by picking up the phone and calling her
office. As you may expect, you probably won't get your senator or representative on the line; in fact, the person you speak
with very well may be a part-time, unpaid college kid who's
happy to be out of class. But most offices will have the courtesy to hear your position, take down your name, and thank
you for your time.

You can also contact your legislators via e-mail. If you know
your senators and House member, simply Google their names
and their websites will come up with contact information on the
home pages. If you don't know who represents you in Congress,
Google "Members of Congress" (or go to www.house.gov/
representatives) to identify your representative, and
Google "Members of the Senate" (or go to www.senate.gov/
general/contact_information/senators_cfm.cfm) to
identify your two senators.

If you're concerned that your single voice won't have any
influence on what your elected official actually decides, you
may be right. But making your opinion known is still crucial
because collective constituent opinion is an important factor
in congressional decision-making. Congressional offices really
do go through the letters from their districts and take note of
what voters are saying. Mail from slick lobbying campaigns
and from crazies are par for the course, but individually
written letters from constituents stand out — and can be
extremely effective tools for expressing your opinion to
policymakers.

Join an Interest Group

Perhaps you want to do more than make the occasional congressional cold call, but you aren't up for devoting your whole life to becoming a Washington insider. That's where interest groups come into play. As we explain in Chapter 3, interest groups are as diverse as the people they represent. Some are collections of giant corporations; others are made up of small businesspeople, or retired persons, or activists for a particular cause. By joining an interest group and paying your dues, you are essentially asking it to advocate on an issue or topic you care about, allowing you to go on living your own life.

Think of it this way: You already have one House member and two senators in Congress who, despite any disagreements you may have with them on particular policy issues, are there to (in theory) represent you. Becoming a member of an interest group is like sending another personal representative into the debate. You already have two knights and a bishop (okay, maybe chess pieces aren't the best analogy for politicians), and now you add a rook and maybe a few pawns. Whereas your congressional representatives may pay little attention to the issues that concern you and may vehemently disagree with you in certain debates, you have the freedom to pick any interest group that aligns with your own point of view.

Be an Activist for a Day

Getting the attention of policymakers can be difficult, especially when they blow past you in a window-tinted Suburban at 50 mph on a residential street. (Obeying speed limits isn't their thing. Nor is paying parking tickets.) That's why some interest groups encourage their members to move beyond just paying dues and become activists.

Activism can take many forms, from sending postcards to stampeding down congressional corridors while being chased by Capitol police (it happens). Some large groups have established events they hold annually in Washington to remind policymakers that they exist and that they command the support of thousands of their constituents. Walks and runs for certain charities are a popular pastime, especially to highlight federal funding to fight certain illnesses, such as leukemia or breast cancer, or certain political issues or causes. For example, every year thousands of activists descend upon Washington for the annual March for Life walk to remind legislators about their antiabortion stance.

Don't be fooled into thinking that activism is only for the fringe crowd that never got over Vietnam. People from all walks of life and with all kinds of political beliefs take on the role of activist. They serve a vital role in focusing policymakers' attention on pressing issues and getting the message out loud and clear that many Americans care deeply about those issues.

Be a Lobbyist for a Day

Lobbying isn't just for the professionals. Anyone can pick up the phone and ask to meet a member of Congress or administration official. Naturally, if these officials accepted every request, they would have very little time to do their real work (like fundraising, a cynic may suspect!). But with a little persistence and a compelling reason, you may be able to squeeze through the door and explain your message to someone on that person's staff. (Since many congressional offices are as crowded as a college dorm room, don't be surprised if your long-awaited meeting ends up taking place in the hallway.)

Interest groups often facilitate amateur lobbying by arranging regular *door knocks* on Capitol Hill. Members volunteer to show up, join a small delegation armed with talking points and briefing materials, and wander from office to office spreading whatever key messages their group wants to share. Don't worry if you're not a lobbying veteran. The truth is, many of the top business executives who go to Capitol Hill to lobby on behalf of their companies are brand new to lobbying as well. Do you belong to a local civic organization that has something to say about federal policy? Consider organizing your own door knock and learning your way around Congress. It's a great excuse for a trip to Washington, especially when the famous cherry blossoms are in bloom.

Submit Public Comments

The United States has developed a remarkably open and transparent system for gathering public input on important policy and regulatory matters. Skim through the *Federal Register,* and you'll find requests for comment on all manner of issues by different executive departments and agencies. A new website, www.regulations.gov, has been created to facilitate the submission of comments in response to many of these public requests. Literally anyone can submit comments. Businesses, nonprofits, citizens, foreigners — a stakeholder is anyone who claims to have a stake in the matter at hand.

Of course, if you want someone to pay attention to your message, it helps to follow a few basic rules. Use a formal letter template and some official stationery, and follow a standard format. Although general comments are always welcome, specific ones that address particular issues policymakers may not have considered can be the most valuable.

Be a Citizen Journalist

Ordinary Americans are playing an increasing role in enhancing political media coverage, which (as we discuss in Chapter 4) plays a major part in how Washington and policymaking function. The easiest way to get started is to launch a blog. Sure, most blogs don't get more than a few curious (or accidental) visitors, and you probably won't be breaking much news (many journalists share this fate), but you can still exercise your constitutional right to speak loud and clear about whatever issues you feel passionately about. Several amateur scribes have even managed to turn their initial online forays into well-paid commentary careers.

Citizen journalism is not limited to typing in your pajamas in your parents' basement. Plenty of strange political behavior has been captured by everyday people with a camera at the ready, and little-known facts have been uncovered by those with far too much time on their hands. Naturally, you don't want to carry this too far and end up like the kid who got a year in prison for hacking into Sarah Palin's e-mail account. But you don't have to commit cybercrime or dig through dumpsters to become an occasional citizen journalist.

Join the Washington Establishment

Maybe you've read this book and thought "That's the life for me." Welcome to the Washington establishment. Joining the club takes hard work, persistence, and luck, but every year countless young folks continue to descend upon Washington to sign up.

It helps to start early. By going to college or graduate school in the Washington area, you can quickly learn your way about the city and start searching for those crucial internships and entry-level jobs on Capitol Hill, in the executive branch, and in the private sector. Young professionals can become influential while still in their 20s. Being in the area can give you a head start in the rat race.

You may find it difficult to get through the door at first. Hill jobs are hard to find, and fresh-faced graduates usually don't start their careers as presidential appointees. Fortunately, where you start doesn't really matter. Thanks to the revolving door, you may move multiple times between the public and private sectors throughout your career. You'll likely don many different hats: staffer, researcher, lobbyist, regulator, lawyer, columnist . . . the list goes on.

Realize that at the end of the day, you're still, in one way or another, contributing to that infinitely intricate and complicated, sometime righteous and often cynical, occasionally dysfunctional but ultimately workable system of government known by all as Washington, D.C.